GREEN NO MORE

London Country Bus Services from beginning to end

Peter Aves

Capital Transport

ACKNOWLEDGEMENTS

After 50 years as a bus enthusiast, including the last 15 with an active involvement in preservation, I have come to know many like-minded people, several of whom have in one way or another made some contribution to this book. I have acknowledged below a few people who have made particular contributions. There are too many others to name, but my thanks go to all of them for their memories of the Country Bus area and their anecdotes and recollections.

Particular thanks must go to my colleagues at Country Bus Rallies. Alan Charman, Colin Rivers and John Huxford have between them an enormous knowledge of London's Country bus network. We all started with 'Green Rovers', some of us more than 50 years ago, and John was apprenticed as a fitter with London Transport after leaving school. Between us we have accumulated thousands of hours riding round almost every route at some time or another. In the last 15 or 20 years, we have also had the opportunity to drive our own buses over so many of the old routes on our running days. Many of their recollections, and no small amount of their knowledge have found their way into this book.

Les Bland, a former conductor and for many years one of our regular run day conductors, passed on several memories of his time at St Albans.

Particular thanks must go to Laurie Akehurst, someone known to many for his own excellent books on London Transport. It was Laurie who also encouraged me when I first mentioned the idea for these books, and who introduced me to Jim Whiting of Capital Transport. 'Driver Aves and Conductor Akehurst' have spent many pleasant days for more than a decade as a regular crew meandering around country lanes in my own RF on running days, me driving, while Laurie issues tickets and gives the passengers his detailed history of the route we're on. Laurie's knowledge of the Country Bus area is unsurpassed, and he has generously passed on a mass of information and detail which has been used in the books, in particular the period up to 1969. David Stewart was very helpful in commenting on and, where necessary, correcting the original captions.

Finally, most thanks of all must go to my wife Christine who knew of my enthusiasm for buses when we met 35 years ago. In the intervening years, she has listened patiently to endless ramblings about Country Bus routes, found space in the house for my collection of timetables, books, models, and a whole host of other bits and pieces, and even enjoyed a few days out on the RF in recent years. She does admit though that my encyclopaedic knowledge of former bus routes is very useful when avoiding endless standing traffic on the M25! This book is written with grateful thanks for her patience over the years.

Contents

Above The 412 from Dorking to Holmbury St Mary and Sutton traversed some narrow hilly roads and was one of the country area's more rural bus routes. Before the War, London Transport established an outstation at Holmbury St Mary, the bus being run by crews who lived in and around the village. Like many others, the route suffered a gradual decline, and in 1975, after further reductions, the outstation was closed. In the early days of London Country, RF 238 runs along the road between Sutton and Holmbury on a journey to Dorking a couple of years before new BNs replaced RFs which had run the route for more than 20 years. It carries the running number DS 1 which was always used for the outstationed bus. A decade later, the route was taken over by Tillingbourne, and a few years after that, London Country's operations from Dorking ended when the garage was closed. (John Miller).

Title page Crawley received a batch of ten new SMs which entered service on 1st August 1970 to replace RTs on town services. The 475 route ran from Northgate across the town to Pease Pottage with a few journeys extended down the A23 to Handcross, and was begun in 1971 when Southdown withdrew their long standing trunk route to Brighton. SM 110 was one of the original batch sent to Leatherhead and was never officially allocated to Crawley, but their unreliability was such that swaps between garages became commonplace. It has arrived at Handcross ready to work back to Crawley. (Barry Le Jeune)

Introduction

I have no recollection of when or why I became interested in buses, but I don't recall a time when I had much interest in any other forms of transport. It was 1964 – I was 15 years old – before my parents owned their first car, and until then, apart from our annual holiday week, family outings were by bus or coach. Dorking and Boxhill were particular favourites of my parents, and since the 712 and 713 Green Line routes passed the end of our road, we would enjoy a day trip out into the Surrey countryside three or four times a year. I was allowed to go on my first Green Rover in 1962, and in the following 30 years I covered just about every country area route. Although passenger numbers were already in serious decline by the early 1960s, I was fortunate to cover all the less frequent rural routes while they still carried reasonable loads.

After London Country took over and began to withdraw many rural routes I covered them again where I could before they disappeared; from St.Albans to Codicote, East Grinstead to Oxted, Hertford to Chapmore End and the last ever 384A journey from Hertford to Great Munden in 1976. With the frequent failure of the newer buses, it would sometimes be possible to catch a ride on an RT or RF, and a well laden RT 994 on a 347 from Garston Garage to Uxbridge in April 1975 was an unexpected treat. The hired Southend PD3s at Harlow and the Royal Blue MWs at Sevenoaks were certainly worth the trip, but the newer types began to hold less interest.

By the mid-1970s, drastic cuts in timetables meant that it became more difficult to plan Rovers even on the more frequent routes, but I continued to travel round the network for a few more years. The vehicles were changing, but the overriding difference was the dramatic reduction in passengers. On a 384 from Hertford one Saturday afternoon in 1978 run by a scruffy RP, we left Hertford Bus Station with just five passengers. We picked up four more in Ware, but the last of them alighted in Dane End, after which (apart from me) the bus ran empty as far as Bennington where we picked up two, plus another one at Walkern. In 1972, a year before the 364 was finally abandoned, I travelled from Hitchin to Luton one Saturday afternoon. There were only a handful of passengers and, other than me, the bus ran empty from Breachwood Green all the way into Luton and perfectly illustrated the reasons why London Country faced such a dire financial position.

This book covers the period from 1970 when London Transport handed over its country bus area to London Country. The next volume will cover the period from the point where the great fleet replacement programme was coming to an end and passenger numbers had peaked, to the end of 1969, by which time the 'Country Area' was effectively bankrupt as a business.

The books have been driven mainly by my own recollections, my fascination for the Country Area's complex scheduling, and how social changes conspired to drastically change the way all bus companies were forced to regard their route networks. The dramatic losses suffered by all operators as passengers deserted buses for cars, and rural village populations dwindled was a country wide problem, but London Transport with its rigid operational approach to its network, were perhaps slower to react than most and never really succeeded in keeping

Chelsham received three BNs from the second batch at the end of 1974 to replace the RFs rostered to the 464, 465 and 485. By this time these routes, like many, were losing heavily – even in 1971 they carried little more than 5000 passengers each week. They were also more costly to operate since – apart from a couple of journeys – buses had to run light from Chelsham to Oxted to take up service. The majority of passengers were carried from Chart and Holland into Oxted, and by 1975 Kent County Council were no longer able to subsidise the sections from Westerham to Crockham Hill and Edenbridge which were in Kent. Surrey though agreed to subsidise a service between Chart and Holland (within the county boundary) so that in 1975, the 465 and 485 were withdrawn. Not long before the route was abandoned, BN 48 descends from Kent Hatch to Crockham Hill on a 465 to Edenbridge. From there it would have worked a 485 to Westerham and a 464 back to Holland, a service pattern which had existed since the routes were altered after the War when the Edenbridge Green Line route was replaced with a bus service. (Colin Fradd)

pace with or managing the decline. Once the political decision had been taken in 1968 to transfer the country area to the National Bus Company, very little was done in terms of long term planning for fleet replacement or any review of a route network which had remained little changed for 25 years.

Over half a century later, the levels of service once operated have long since gone and it is difficult to recall now that they ever existed. The main trunk routes which had linked London suburbs with the outer edges of the country area were all gradually cut back and the lesser routes were either abandoned or reduced to skeleton timetables. Those that did remain eventually had to be paid for by public subsidy since they could never run at a profit.

The first of my own countless Green Rovers was 55 years ago, and the last almost 30 years ago. During that period, I saw the slow demise of an era which would never return. I am only glad I had the chance to experience it all when I did.

Peter Aves
April 2017

1   The Poisoned Chalice: 1970-1976

Opposite The 360 would have been ideal to convert to omo when Luton received new Atlanteans in 1972 for the 321. To convert the 360 to omo however would have meant extending the running time such that the crew operated timetable requiring one bus would have meant two omo buses to maintain the same 30 minute headway; thus crew operation was retained and the 360 retained an isolated RT allocation. RTs were replaced by SNBs in 1976, although crew operation was retained to avoid the additional costs of a second bus, but was shortlived as the route was transferred to United Counties in December that year prior to Luton garage closing at the end of January 1977. Soon after London Country took over, RT 4044 is in Luton Town centre (Alan Osborne)

The history of London Country Bus Services and the network it inherited on 1st January 1970 has been the subject of a number of excellent books, and many of the details do not need to be repeated in this one. The business as it existed when London Country took over could only be described in financial management terms as a 'basket case'. It had a level of fixed overheads which the business could not support, its passengers were deserting in increasing numbers, it had un-sustainable daily running costs, an out-of-date fleet, and was simply unviable. The urgent need was to reduce costs while at the same time invest heavily in new vehicles, but given that no reserves or cash had been carried forward from London Transport, any capital had to be borrowed. Even the Minister of Transport reported early in 1970 that losses of over £1 million had to be budgeted for in London Country's first two years alone, and by any normal commercial criteria, no bank or investor would continue to support such a loss making business. The company's problems were acute, but they were by no means alone amongst National Bus Company (NBC) subsidiaries, and it is first worth setting the scene which prevailed across the country at the end of 1969 to provide the context in which the NBC had to operate at the time.

Many of the former Tilling and BET Group companies had route networks with proportions of rural mileage much greater than London Country, and in areas where the population was far more sparse than the Home Counties. The Unions had been implacable in their resistance to extending one-man operation in the late 1960s, and all operators had suffered delays with endless and often fruitless negotiations in their efforts to reduce costs by increasing the proportion of omo working. By 1967, only 8% of the then Tilling Group's total mileage was one-man operated, and although a much greater proportion of the rural mileage had been converted, crew operation of many journeys on rural routes was still common-place. Progress towards more one-man conversions was accelerating but even by the end of 1969 the overall total had risen to only around 20% of all mileage run.

In extreme cases, such as that in 1968 with United at their Carlisle depot, which ran some extremely rural mileage, the Company eventually had to threaten complete closure of that depot unless staff were prepared to extend omo. Progress by Ribble, who had the largest presence in Carlisle (it was also their fourth largest depot) was appallingly slow and, in January 1969, of 102 drivers only six were rostered to one-man duties. Although Ribble operated all the City services, there was much rural mileage from Carlisle, the majority of which was still crew operated, and only after a long battle with staff was full omo finally achieved in June 1972. To pay for this over-manning, fare increases in 1970 and 1971 had been so swingeing that for some local journeys within the City, taxi fares became cheaper than Ribble's buses! In spring 1971, the rural network was decimated, and in three years from 1969 to 1972, the platform staff had shrunk from 260 down to 110. In the face of falling passengers, Union intransigence combined with lethargic management had reduced service levels, in some cases to just skeleton timetables, and had driven away yet more passengers.

In 1969 Eastern Counties carried out a survey of its East Suffolk Area. Their main Suffolk depot was at Ipswich which had a total allocation of almost 100 buses, roughly a third of which were outstationed all over Suffolk in small towns and villages in various small sheds and yards, and ran over 50 separate bus routes. So complex were the schedules that only eight of these routes ran to the same timetable each weekday, the rest having combinations of journeys on different days based around Market Days and shopping. Some routes had as little as two or three journeys each week – two routes had just one – and served some of Suffolk's most remote areas. It was no surprise therefore that apart two inter-urban routes from Ipswich, the survey found that the entire East Suffolk area was financially unviable. The situation across their Norfolk and Cambridge areas was no different, although the city services in Norwich, Peterborough and Cambridge provided some profit.

In 1970, Crosville concluded that no fewer than 200 of its rural routes were unprofitable. Faced with a continuing drop in passengers of 10% per annum, Crosville stated that they could no longer operate these routes without some form of financial assistance. To have abandoned them would have meant the complete loss of bus services to many country towns, the closure of nine rural depots, and the loss of 275 vehicles and 700 staff. In rural Wales with lower levels of car ownership, such an outcome would have been disastrous, and few of the 700 staff shed would have easily found re-employment in such an area.

Even in Devon and Cornwall with its large influx of summer visitors, Western and Southern National had similar problems. Following a review of its loss making routes, five small depots and outstations were all closed in late 1971 and many rural services wholly or partly withdrawn. Timetables on many other routes were cut back in the spring of 1972 when no fewer than 60 vehicles became surplus to requirements, and many platform staff lost their jobs.

These were not isolated cases, as route networks everywhere outside urban areas were equally precarious. Clearly this could not continue without either mass withdrawals and loss of jobs, or the provision of widespread financial assistance in some form. This assistance had been enshrined in the 1968 Transport Act which allowed local authorities to provide subsidy for bus services which were 'socially necessary'. This though was not defined, and although local authorities were empowered to provide subsidies, Government failed to recognize that local authorities had no real understanding of how the bus industry operated, nor did they have the right staff to manage what would become a deluge of urgent applications for funds. Local politics also meant widely differing attitudes to giving taxpayer's money to bus companies whether 'socially necessary' or otherwise, so there were many inconsistencies in the way funding was provided.

Apart from the provision of financial support, the 1968 Transport Act also compelled the National Bus Company to *'maintain a balance of revenue over expenditure'*. To achieve this, fare increases were needed for operators to maintain even a reduced level of services, but the Traffic Commissioners at the time felt constrained by Government policy, under the aegis of the Prices and Incomes Board, and took the view that *'the Public Interest'* demanded the lowest possible fare increases, and that any increase should be trimmed to balance an operator's income against expenditure. Matching *'income and expenditure'* was of course the exact opposite of the requirement of the Transport Act for the NBC to make a surplus. This was a masterly piece of woolly headed politics, and an outstanding example of the principle of 'unintended consequences' which failed to recognise that *'the Public Interest'* would hardly be best served by the mass withdrawal of great swathes of the country's rural bus network, and no small increase in unemployment from all the drivers, conductors, engineering and support staff who would lose their jobs. With declining passenger numbers and high inflation, to limit fare increases to a balance of income and expenditure did nothing but strip away an operator's already depleted cash reserves, even if any existed, which in London Country's case they did not.

The 462 had originally been cut back from Staines to Chertsey in the 1966 winter schedules, and apart from a few peak journeys to Chertsey, cut further back to Addlestone two years later, but when the main 436 timetable to Staines was reduced to hourly in 1974, the daytime 462 timetable was extended back to Staines to compensate. The route was quite rural for much of its length however, and would suffer dramatic timetable cuts to offset heavy losses, but prior to this sometime in 1974, SM 465 in original livery comes along the road between Fetcham and Stoke D'Abernon on a Staines working. (Colin Fradd)

After the last GS workings on the 309/309A were converted to RF in February 1969, Garston retained GS 33 and 42 for the 336A until the route was finally withdrawn in March 1972. All that remained by then were five morning journeys, one at lunchtime and six from mid-afternoon with the final departure from Rickmansworth at 6.49pm for the last commuters from London. One delightful oddity until the end however was a single morning journey to Northwood and back, and on 6th July 1971, GS 42 waits by the Estate Office at Loudwater Village before setting off on this. (Author)

Even before absorbing London Country, the NBC had warned that it could not meet the financial targets set for it by central Government whilst still maintaining services at their 1968/69 levels. In March 1970, new regulations limiting driver's hours came into force, cutting the working week, and NBC reckoned that this alone would cost £1million in its first year, coming at precisely a time when major economies were necessary. In September 1970 therefore, the NBC announced that it was compelled to further reduce the burden of loss making services, and that the age-old practice of cross subsidisation was now no longer acceptable. The growth of car ownership continued to erode the number of remaining passengers who supported loss making rural services, and the burden on fares for those passengers using urban services, the profit from which had been used to subsidise the rural routes, had become too great to sustain. The Group felt compelled therefore to instruct its subsidiaries to reduce this burden by announcing the complete withdrawal of all loss making services after reasonable notice, *'to the extent that it is necessary to restore the overall financial position'.*

In this context therefore, London Country's problems can be seen as part of the nationwide decline described above, but it does not detract from the very serious special issues which it had to face in 1970. Apart from the financial losses common to almost all NBC companies, its particular problem was the age of its fleet, which was the greatest in the NBC, and the operational issues resulting from a route network which at one end of the spectrum had several loss making rural services, and at the other operated in some of the worst traffic congestion anywhere, which caused untold disruption to schedules. The former culture of London Transport's long held rigid operating methods had also done nothing to contribute to the radical changes that were necessary.

The 409 had been one of the major Country Area trunk routes but declined greatly from the late 1960s. South of East Grinstead, passenger loadings were low, and it was a perfect example of a route suitable for omo double deckers much earlier had the right buses been purchased. In the end, it would be 1977 before SNBs converted the 409 but in 1971, in London Country's attractive livery, RML 2332 stops in East Grinstead high street on a journey to Forest Row.
(Mike Harris)

The 420 was introduced in 1950 to provide a link from the new estate at Sheerwater to Woking, and was soon extended to West Byfleet. During the 1960s, the timetable was steadily reduced and before London Country took over all that remained was a skeleton peak hour and schools service. The route did not require lowbridge buses but was mostly interworked from Addlestone's RLH allocation. Apart from two months at Godstone in 1958 to cover for buses away on overhaul, RLH 32 spent its entire 18 year life at either Addlestone or Guildford. Not long before withdrawal, it is turning at West Byfleet and looks very well after a long life. It was in service on the last day of RLHs and then stored at Garston for a few months. After sale to a dealer it eventually became part of the 'Timebus' heritage fleet in Watford where it is still in use.
(Geoff Rixon)

The aged fleet was a result of London Transport's lack of sufficient forward planning in its vehicle replacement programme, and in the end doing too little too late. The much vaunted *'Reshaping London's Buses'* plan which London Transport had produced in 1966 had placed great emphasis on shorter routes using high capacity single deckers, and with a significant extension to one-man operation. Earlier in 1964, the *'Phelps Brown Report'* had, amongst other matters, come from Union claims for higher wages, and whilst largely supporting the Union's case, the report had also concluded that there should be a widespread acceptance of one-man operation in return for higher rates of pay.

The reshaping plan concentrated almost entirely on the Central Area, with only passing reference to the Country Area and Green Line to the effect that one man operation would be extended. The main result of the plan for high capacity single deckers was the large fleet of AEC Merlin MBs and MBSs, and later the even larger fleet of AEC Swift SMs and SMSs, but despite the proposals of the Phelps-Brown report – which Unions had accepted in principle – progress towards greater one-man operation was severely delayed by continued Union intransigence through the second half of the 1960s. Despite all this, there had nevertheless been an apparent lack of urgency on the part of London Transport in the Country Bus department to push forward with more one-man conversions, and the introduction of more suitable buses.

The MBs and MBSs which had eventually come into service from the end of 1968 were only a small part of a necessary solution in the Country Area. The purchase of 100 RMLs in 1965/66 had been the wrong choice for fleet replacement. By then the Atlantean and Fleetline had become well established amongst many operators, and when omo operation of double deckers became legal in 1966, those companies who had such buses could begin to convert routes to omo. Whilst agreements with Unions were often difficult and protracted, at least the right buses were already in service. Geoffrey Fernyhough who was London Transport's Country Area general manager (and who moved on to the same post with London Country) at least had the foresight to understand that the RML – excellent though it was – was not the right choice at the time. His objections however were overruled at Board level, and the standard Routemaster was purchased, the only concession being the small batch of eight Fleetlines which were purchased more as an experiment to test them in service than for future one-manning, and went to East Grinstead for the 424. Even with the delays in reaching Union agreements, if the RMLs had instead been rear engined Fleetlines, then the country bus fleet could have had perhaps one hundred omo-suitable double deckers in service at least a year before London Country took over as opposed to the solitary batch of XFs. Indeed, London Transport's tardy approach to pushing through one-manning of double deckers meant that even these buses on route 424 were still crew operated when London Country took over.

The three XFs which had been repainted and sent to Stevenage for the innovative 'Blue Arrow' services on 28th December 1969, were the first double deckers to run without a conductor, although they used fareboxes rather than driver collection of fares. These had been replaced by three Central Area XA Atlanteans, but these eight buses at East Grinstead remained crew worked until London Country pushed through the change in June 1970 at the same time as the SMs came into service to begin replacing RTs.

XF 6 looks immaculate in the blue and silver 'Blue Arrow' livery as it stops in Gunnells Wood Road in the Stevenage industrial area on a journey to Chells on the eastern edge of the town. These innovative routes paved the way for a complete network of services linking Stevenage's expanding housing areas to the town and main employment centre to the west. (John Boylett)

Reigate was the first garage to put MBs in service in March 1968 when they replaced the main RF workings on the 447. It was also the first to put standee MBSs into service in November that year when the 430 local route was converted from RT. Illustrating both types, MBS 419 awaits a replacement driver at Red Cross in Reigate on a 430 to Merstham, with MB 91 behind on route 447. The MB has been repainted into NBC livery while the MBS still retains its London Country version. The roads through Batts Hill estate on the 447 were far more difficult to navigate with MBs than the RFs they replaced, the extra width, long wheelbase and long overhangs making tight corners and gaps between parked cars very difficult. The original MBs had the lower driving position compared to the MBS, the difference between the two being obvious in this picture, and the lower position was unpopular with drivers. Both types began to be replaced at Reigate by new Leyland Nationals towards the end of 1974, but it was a further three years before it operated its last one. (Capital Transport collection)

On 1st January 1970, London Country's total scheduled Monday to Friday run out was 1,122, of which 643 were crew operated double deckers, 437 were elderly RTs, the oldest of which were even then 22 years old. On Saturdays crew buses numbered 452 out of a total of 856, and on Sundays 164 out of a total of 389. That 42% of the Sunday schedules were still worked by crewed buses was perhaps the most telling statistic in terms of the financial burden then being carried, and the lack of progress made by London Transport before London Country took over. There were plenty of crew operated double deck routes which could have been converted in 1968/1969 had Fleetlines been purchased, but by 1970, the need for cost savings had become so great that almost every double deck route needed to be converted, regardless of how busy it might be at certain times of the day. With such a high proportion of crewed buses still scheduled for service, the continuing cost of so many conductors was a burden which was simply unaffordable. One of London Country's earliest announcements therefore was that the entire network would be converted to one-man operation, a process which in the event would take the whole of the decade to complete.

The first priority had to be to acquire as many new buses as possible as quickly as possible. In this regard at least some early progress could be made as a result of the 1969 order by London Transport for 138 dual entrance AEC Swifts, which were the last Country Area orders from the Reshaping Plan. The first batch of 48 arrived in June 1970, and all were used to replace crew-operated double deckers. Some went to Crawley for town services, some to Leatherhead, and the rest to Addlestone and Guildford to replace the lowbridge RLHs and convert the routes from Guildford through Woking to Walton and Staines to omo, which for some years had become less important and where few journeys still warranted two-man operation. The 16 RLHs still scheduled were all 18 or 20 years old, and the new SMs were a much needed replacement. The sunken gangway lowbridge double decker was a design that had been superseded almost twenty years earlier, and by the time the RLHs ran for the last time on 31st July 1970, there were few similar buses remaining anywhere across the country. There was a certain irony however that, despite London Country's aged fleet, London Transport had to keep a small batch of its RLHs in service in east London on the 178 route until the following April pending delivery of new single deckers.

The remaining 90 SMs began to arrive early in 1971 with the first of them going to Amersham and High Wycombe to convert RT routes, the result of which was that Amersham became the first garage to be entirely converted to one-man operation. This converted the long 353 route from Berkhamsted to Windsor but, although Amersham ran almost the entire allocation, Windsor retained its crew working on the first trip to Berkhamsted each morning, returning to Windsor just before 11.00am. With a 30-minute layover in the morning at Berkhamsted the Windsor crew duty was a very easy one indeed, carrying minimal mid-morning passengers on the return trip, and continued until late 1973. Unusually, the end to end running time on the 353 was not increased to account for omo conversion, and this probably reflected more about what had become an over-generous timetable for crew operation, rather than the need to allow for slower boarding times with omo. Although the 353 maintained a number of useful links, it passed through some of the most affluent parts of the Home Counties, car ownership having stripped away the bulk of its passengers, and would have been an obvious target for conversion in 1968/69 had the right buses been available.

Up to this point, the SMs had been allocated to secondary routes which in general were less busy or arduous, but at the same time as the Amersham conversions, a batch was sent to Hatfield to replace RMCs on the 303/303A, a long and busy route. The previous end-to-end running time of 1hr 55mins from Barnet to Hitchin was increased by only six minutes on conversion to omo, and with only seven minutes' layover at the Hitchin end, there was no real recovery time in the event of late running. With frequent stops and high loadings, the SMs had to be driven hard to maintain time, and experience would soon show that with their relatively small engines and limited performance under load, they were simply not up to the job on what was still one of the Country Area's most important trunk routes. Indeed, their performance on the 303/303A was so much of a concern that they lasted only two years until February 1973 when they were all moved on to

Harlow received SM 458 and 515 in October 1972 specifically for the 812. This was an express service running only on Monday to Friday to a 20 minute headway with just six stops to provide a direct link from Potter Street on the old road through Harlow Village to the railway. SM 515 displays the blue blinds used for Express services, as it waits at Harlow Town Station to work back to Potter Street. The flat fare notice is prominent and the farebox is visible inside the bus. The timetable required both buses, and without a spare SM their unreliability soon made operation of the route difficult to maintain. (Ian Pringle)

less testing work. The SMs were also a poor substitute for the RMCs they replaced at Hatfield which had comfortable seats and platform doors, but the overriding necessity had to be cost savings. At the same time as the changeover at Hatfield, the first of the Croydon trunk routes saw a partial conversion as the 'country' section of the 403 was converted to SM. The route number 403A was used for the service between Croydon and Tonbridge, and Chelsham's RTs were confined after the change to the urban section between Wallington and Warlingham Park or Farleigh. Although the 403A had some busier sections – particularly between Westerham and Sevenoaks, and into and out of Tonbridge, it was a further example of a route which could have been converted to omo much earlier if the right buses had been purchased.

Dunton Green received their first SMs in July 1971. In February the following year I clearly recall a heavily loaded journey on SM 530 on a 454 from Tonbridge to Sevenoaks one Saturday lunchtime when the bus was still quite new. There is a long steep climb up from Sevenoaks Weald village, and by the time the bus made the summit, there was smoke and the smell of burning oil coming from under the rear seat where I sat. We arrived at Sevenoaks Bus Station with the overheating buzzer still sounding and the bus was promptly replaced with the spare RF parked there, presumably for just such a situation!

The conversions at Amersham and High Wycombe brought the SMs onto the 362/362A and what was one of the most arduous hills anywhere in the network. Amersham Hill out of High Wycombe up to Hazlemere was both long and in places steep, and the SMs struggled with the heavy loads which were still common-place over this section of the route. In a relatively short time, the SMs developed a reputation for overheating and a general lack of robustness when compared to RTs, RMs and RFs. The sight of a failed SM by the roadside with a seat cushion propped up against the rear panel became a not infrequent occurrence, and this lack of reliability would overshadow most new buses throughout the 1970s.

New SMs went to Hatfield in February 1971 to convert the 303/303A and the text refers to their unsuitability for such a long, busy route. When the first Leyland Nationals went to Hatfield in February 1973, they replaced MBs which in turn displaced the SMs after only two years so that they could be redeployed on less demanding routes. The MBs proved much more suitable and on 28th July 1973, MB 83 pulls away from the stop outside Potters Bar garage on a 303A to Hitchin. Assuming the MB is on time, then RP 18 behind on a 716 to Hitchin is 15 minutes late – a common occurrence on most journeys out of London. (Mike Harris)

At the same time as Amersham's double deck routes were converted to omo, its remaining Green Line route was withdrawn from London and cut back to run only as far as Uxbridge. Thus the 710 effectively became just a limited stop rail link service to connect with the Underground at Uxbridge, and Amersham's Green Line allocation had gone from 11 crew RFs plus duplicates before the 703 was withdrawn in November 1964 to just two omo RFs for what remained of the 710. Given that Amersham itself also had a frequent rail link to central London, the 710 only provided a facility for passengers from the Chalfonts who might want to go to London, and in reality these would drive the short distance to Gerrards Cross and catch a train. The truncated 710 was therefore a lost cause, and the only surprise was that the remaining timetable lasted another 18 months before final withdrawal in September 1972, severing Amersham's last association with Green Line operations.

The new SMs made only a small impression on the urgent need for new buses. London Country soon placed orders for large numbers of Leyland Atlanteans, and for 90 AEC Reliances which would have coach seating and would convert all the remaining crew operated Green Line routes. At the beginning of 1970, Green Line schedules still required 39 RCL and 43 RMC, and the Reliances were to be used to replace all of these, allowing the Routemaster coaches to replace RTs on bus routes. By 1970, 18 RMCs were already allocated as buses, having been made redundant from Green Line routes before London Country took over, and the remaining 82 newer RMCs and RCLs that were to be displaced by the Reliance coaches would make welcome replacements for the much older RTs.

The first four Routemasters were placed in service by London Transport in 1956-58, each to a slightly different specification to test them in service. The third was designated CRL 4 (coach-Routemaster-Leyland) and was London Transport's only double decker with a body by ECW. It was tested on a number of Green Line routes and succeeded where previous double deck coaches had not, in that further vehicles of similar design followed. The bus was re-designated RMC 4 and was demoted to bus routes in 1968 when many of the class became surplus following cuts to Green Line schedules. It spent its remaining life at Hatfield, and is seen here in South Hatfield on a short working of the 341 from St Albans. It was Hatfield's last Routemaster, not being withdrawn until May 1979, and even spent a day on the Hitchin to London Green Line route covering for a failed RP. After withdrawal it went to Dorking as a 'showbus', and was retained for occasional special duties. (Mike Harris)

Apart from new orders, the initial need for new buses was so great that London Country trawled other NBC subsidiaries for unwanted buses and for orders that could be diverted to them. More AEC Swifts were acquired including a batch which materialised in March 1972 as the SMA class which was diverted from South Wales Transport and had odd shaped Alexander semi-coach bodies. These were put to work on the 725 Green Line route to replace RFs. In the end, most of the batch spent their entire and fairly short working lives on the 725, and although theoretically better than the RFs they replaced, suffered from the same mechanical shortcomings as the other Swifts. They had particularly ineffective heating systems and the limited performance of their engines – like the bus version – was a disadvantage on a suburban service with an end-to-end running time of almost three and a half hours in constant heavy traffic. In warm weather they became uncomfortably hot, and also provided somewhat cramped leg room. Despite their replacement, RFs continued to perform regularly on the 725, two still being in regular use on the route six years later when, though 27 years old, they could still be relied upon to put in a trouble-free day's work on Green Line duties through heavy traffic, and were still capable of being driven hard to maintain time – a feat that their replacements so often failed to achieve. Although they were a necessity as part of the fleet replacement, the SMAs were so unsatisfactory that they only outlasted the last RFs on the 725 by a short period before they too were replaced by new heavyweight Reliances.

The SMAs spent almost their whole life on the 725 and SMA 6 is loading in Windsor at the start of a journey to Gravesend when relatively new in its original London Country livery. With their cramped leg room and unpredictable heating systems, they were not particularly comfortable, and were no more reliable than the SM buses. In less than seven years, most had been replaced by new RB class coaches and by the middle of 1980 only five of the original 21 remained in service. Throughout their short lives, RFs regularly substituted for them on the 725, outlasting them in the end. (Peter Plummer)

Following NBC's instructions 'to restore the overall financial balance', in 1970 London Country had made it clear to all the local authorities in its area that without subsidies, loss making routes would have to be withdrawn. Indeed, London Country's warning was quite unequivocal and, in October 1970, gave authorities three months in which to respond with their proposals. The whole issue of public subsidies for 'socially necessary' bus routes – especially those which were unprofitable – was still in its infancy and as has been mentioned, most authorities were ill equipped to deal with such demands. To confuse the issue further, the Transport Act referred to subsidising services which were of benefit to people in rural areas, but did not define 'rural'. Finally, in any given area, financial support could come from County Councils or District Councils (or both) 'as they saw fit', and this allowed the more reluctant councils to delay or do nothing, so that initially there was a general lack of guidance or collective thinking on the part of councils everywhere across the Country. The principal problem was that Government legislation – whilst well intentioned in principle – was, as is often the case, poorly thought through in terms of the details to actually make it work and provide bus operators with financial support. The procrastination of many councils was understandable in the circumstances, but it did nothing for the NBC's subsidiaries who had hundreds of loss-making rural services which simply could not continue in their present form, if at all.

As well as the 135 SMs delivered in 1970 and 1971, 15 more were acquired from South Wales. They had Willowbrook bodies and were classified SMW, the 'W' simply indicating Wales The first three had seen service in Wales for a short period, and had dual door bodywork. They spent their entire life at Crawley, and SMW 1 is at Crawley bus station waiting to work to Pease Pottage. The 475 had partly replaced Southdown's 23 service when they withdrew from Crawley in April 1971 and included a few journeys further down the A23 to Handcross, a couple of which were rostered for RT operation. (Author)

The other 12 SMWs had not seen service previously and were diverted by NBC to London Country to assist with the dire need for new buses. They all went to St Albans where they converted some lesser crew routes to omo, displacing RTs. One of these was the irregular 338 to Harperbury Hospital near Radlett where SMW 10 has just arrived at the terminus. (John Miller)

The 317 was an infrequent rural route whose timetable was greatly reduced in the early 1970s, but survived the cuts of 1973 as it did not run into Bedfordshire. RF 564 is about to cross the river Gade at Great Gaddesden on a journey back to its home garage. The newer blinds showed Gt Gaddesden Cross Roads as an intermediate point presumably to avoid passengers assuming the route went via the village centre, which was 200 yards from the cross roads! It was withdrawn from Hemel Hempstead in September 1975, being sold for scrap to Booth's at Rotherham a few months later. (Colin Fradd)

In London Country's area, Surrey were foremost in commissioning a study of their own and would in time become one of the better organised and supportive councils. Surrey's own survey in early 1971 had identified that about three quarters of its adult population owned a car, and equally importantly that only one third of all households had no car and therefore relied on public transport. Hertfordshire gave positive early responses together with a willingness to co-ordinate the efforts of some of the District Councils in the county. Of the remainder, there was a general lack of both co-ordination and commitment, with Bedfordshire and Buckinghamshire being particularly reluctant, although some of the District Councils in these areas came forward with promises of support for specific routes.

Against this background, in the first few months of 1971, London Country looked critically at all its rural services, and in Hertfordshire alone it identified no fewer than 22 loss-making routes. These comprised the entire rural network from Hertford (including the links to Stevenage, Welwyn Garden City and Harlow), two rural services from Hemel Hempstead (317/317A to Berkhamsted and 337 to Dunstable), and other very infrequent routes such as the 381 (Toothill–Epping–Harlow) and 807 (Stevenage–Weston–Letchworth). Even more important services such as the 335 and 336 which linked Watford to Amersham, Slough and Windsor were losing money and were included in the list. The losses though were by no means confined to Hertfordshire, and the review threw up many more routes which could not continue without support.

By the middle of 1971, some clear idea began to emerge as to the levels of funding that might be available from local authorities. Whilst Hertfordshire were generally supportive, they declined to fund some routes, and so the 329, 381, 807, and the 351 Buntingford rail replacement service were all withdrawn completely on 7th August. Only four years earlier, the 381 had run six journeys to Toothill from Epping and ten through Epping Green but had suffered drastic losses in passengers. Even before London Country took over, the Saturday service to Toothill had dropped to just two morning journeys, the Epping Green service had been halved and the route was completely unsustainable without subsidy. In its last year of operation the 807 consisted of just one works journey and one afternoon shopping journey during the week, and bizarrely one Saturday afternoon journey into Stevenage with no return trip, so that its final demise was inevitable and probably missed by nobody. When the 351 had begun in November 1964, it had run nine journeys to both Much Hadham and Buntingford, but its potential to maintain the link to London for rail passengers had always been tenuous, so that by August 1971 all that remained were one evening and two morning trips to Much Hadham, and two each morning and early evening to Buntingford. The decline of the 329 had been equally dramatic. Until the cuts of winter 1965, there were eight journeys to Knebworth on Saturday, five Wednesday, and three Monday, Thursday and Friday. After those cuts, the service was reduced to five journeys on Saturday, and to three on Wednesdays, with the remaining service unchanged except for Tuesday replacing Thursday with journeys via Datchworth village after the link to Hitchin was withdrawn. This survived three more years, but in the winter 1968 cuts was reduced to just three journeys Tuesday, Friday and Saturday only, plus two Wednesday morning journeys only as far as Datchworth for Hertford Market day. It is a measure of the decline in shopping traffic that the Market Day service failed and was soon withdrawn, so that by the time London Country took over, the three remaining journeys running on only three days a week were losing heavily.

The local service from Hertford to Ware Park Hospital was numbered 333B until the suffix was discontinued in 1974. It survived the cuts in 1971, but the timetable had been successively cut back from the six afternoon journeys for visiting times plus early and late journeys for staff. The Saturday service and the last two Sunday afternoon journeys were withdrawn in June 1974 and, on 27th August 1974, RF 243 waits outside the hospital on one of the two remaining staff journeys. The service was finally abandoned completely in May 1976. The hospital itself has also long since closed and been converted to flats. (Mike Harris)

The long established 410 route was converted to omo in February 1972 with a batch of Daimler Fleetlines diverted from an order by Western Welsh. Classified AF, they proved more reliable than many other new buses and spent more than 10 years on this long arduous route. They were delivered in London Country green and yellow livery but were all later repainted, and here AF 9 in NBC corporate livery runs into Bromley on a journey from Reigate (Peter Plummer)

In the southern area, even routes once as important as the cross country 410 linking towns and villages across Surrey and Kent to Bromley and Reigate had become marginal, with several loss making journeys during the day and evenings. The sections from Biggin Hill into Bromley, and locally into Redhill and Reigate took enough fares, but although Godstone, Oxted and Westerham had once provided good loads, these had seriously declined and the otherwise open countryside most of the way from Bletchingley to Biggin Hill meant by 1970 few stops and fewer passengers. Some journeys still warranted double deckers, and this was one of the routes which could have been converted to omo much earlier had the right buses been available. Having managed to divert an order for 11 new Daimler Fleetlines from Western Welsh, they were ideal for the route and entered service in February 1972, making the 410 the first important trunk route to be converted to one-man double deckers. In those days, before the M25 had been built, traffic along the old A25 was often heavy with frequent congestion through Westerham. With a new timetable and passengers unfamiliar with having to pay the driver, the first day – Saturday 19th February – was something of a shambles. The former daytime end-to-end running time of 1hr 40mins was extended by only seven minutes which was optimistic, so that timekeeping would be difficult anyway. The 9.51am from Reigate on that Saturday morning departed 38 minutes late, and by midday the new timetable had become meaningless. For years, the 410 had connected at Westerham with the 403 and the 485, and these connections were completely lost. But, despite the initial problems, the main objective had been achieved, and later that year in July when the 410 Sunday service was abandoned, the spare buses were used to convert the 411. Then, apart from a single crew duty on the 709 Green Line, Godstone no longer rostered conductors on Sundays.

London Country's southern network was for the most part less rural and lost less money than in Hertfordshire and the Chilterns, but the infrequent 494 from East Grinstead to Oxted was withdrawn in July 1973. In north Kent, the routes south from Dartford and Gravesend were completely revised with the section from Longfield to West Kingsdown on the 452 abandoned in February 1971, together with the Saturday evening service on the other rural routes. Up to the point when it was withdrawn, the two-hourly timetable on the 452 had remained virtually unchanged since the route had been started in May 1934 – perhaps an outstanding example of London Transport's inflexible approach in the face of changing travel patterns. Of the other rural routes in the area, the 489A to Meopham, and 451/490 to Hartley Court were completely abandoned in January 1972, the service through New Barn and Westwood being virtually halved at the same time. The 413/413A routes were Dunton Green's most rural operation, the 413A to Four Elms having already gone before London Country took over. The section from Sevenoaks to Ide Hill was just about viable but beyond here, along the single track lane to Toys Hill and down to Brasted, carried almost nobody. On 7th October 1970, I travelled on RF 239 working the 1.58pm from Brasted, and apart from myself, not one single passenger was picked up until two boarded at Ide Hill. Even by the time Sevenoaks was reached, only three more passengers had joined, one at Bayleys Hill and two more at Cross Keys on the edge of Sevenoaks itself. This was all too typical of loadings on rural services, and it was inevitable that the Brasted to Ide Hill section was abandoned in January 1972 at the same time as the North Kent routes above. The remaining section from Sevenoaks to Ide Hill was joined with the 404 to form one route from Shoreham to Ide Hill, and with Sevenoaks then in the centre of the route, the revised service was just about worthwhile. In September 1971, Maidstone & District cut back their route 55 (Sevenoaks – Seal – Kemsing), and London Country diverted some journeys on the 421 to the quaintly named Noah's Ark Estate in Kemsing as part replacement. Of all these routes the only replacement was a Post Bus service between Lingfield and Oxted over the 494 route consisting of just a couple of journeys timed more to suit postal deliveries than the needs of the occasional shopping trip into Oxted.

After the reductions on the rural routes in north Kent in 1972, the service via Westwood to Longfield and Ash was abandoned. A year later, the service to Hartley Court went, and all that remained was an hourly service via New Barn and Longfield to New Ash Green and Ash Village. If it were not for the development of a 'new village' at New Ash Green, it is likely that there would have been no service south of Longfield at all, and sometime in 1974 BN 24 comes along the road from Longfield working a journey to New Ash Green. (Colin Fradd)

After omo conversion, the 421 timetable retained one short journey from Sevenoaks to Otford at 6.39am on Saturday morning. It was scheduled to be worked by a Green Line coach before its day's work on the 705, and RP 70 repainted into NBC livery turns round Otford Pond on this working. (Colin Fradd)

In Surrey, London Country was not alone in needing to cut services, despite the County Council's more proactive approach to funding. In the six years following their takeover of the 448 route, Tillingbourne's network had suffered dramatic losses in passenger numbers, and during 1971 the business moved from profit to loss. Surrey was not able to support its remaining Guildford Town service to Warren Road so that Tillingbourne withdrew it completely in October 1971. Another Guildford independent – Safeguard – took over the route but withdrew after only seven weeks. The former 448 to Peaslake was cut back to a 90-minute headway on Saturdays so that it could be worked by only one bus, and although Surrey continued to subsidise the Sunday service, it too had to be abandoned in late 1972. The rapid decline of this route from needing four buses to work a 30-minute headway all day to just two buses in the week, one on Saturday and none Sunday, was a prime example of the effects of increasing affluence and car ownership in the Home Counties. Tillingbourne's GSs were by now increasingly difficult to keep running, and a number of former Western National Bristol LS and SU saloons were purchased. The LS was more powerful and performed better on the hilly terrain than the SU, but was not ideal on the narrow section of the 448 from Gomshall up to Burrows Cross. Tillingbourne even purchased two RFs (595 and 649) and a double decker for school runs, but the school work was soon lost as the fleet and service levels became unreliable through lack of funds. In April 1972, North Downs Rural Transport at Forest Green (who had purchased the routes from Brown Motor Services) suddenly ceased trading. They too were suffering losses on the route into Horsham and that to Guildford which paralleled London Country's 425 from Abinger Hammer. They had run out of sufficient funds to maintain the fleet, and the Ministry of Transport's inspectors finally served prohibition notices on the buses, giving them no option but to cease running. McCann's Forest Green garage took over the routes (despite objections from Tillingbourne and London Country), a development which would lead indirectly to fundamental changes along the Guildford to Dorking corridor of London Country's routes over the next decade.

Whereas Hertfordshire and Surrey were supportive from the beginning, Bedfordshire took little notice of London Country's warnings that loss-making services would be withdrawn, and declined to offer any support to their rural routes running into the county, of which the 337 from Hemel Hempstead to Dunstable was the principal route, running every two hours six days a week. With no support from Bedfordshire, in February 1972 London Country simply cut back the 337 to Studham which was just over the county boundary from Hertfordshire. The 352 still ran a few journeys from Dunstable to Dagnall on Wednesday, Friday and Saturday, but since these were run using the bus from the 337 they were abandoned at the same time. This severed Dagnall's remaining link to Dunstable, but was partly covered later when United Counties diverted some journeys on their Luton to Aylesbury route. The 364A from Luton ran just into Hertfordshire for a short distance before running back into Bedfordshire from Markyate up to Kensworth, buses also running some works journeys from Whipsnade and Studham into Dunstable on the 337 and 343A. These too were all abandoned, London Country even cutting out the small diversion round Woodside village, just inside Bedfordshire, on the way to Markyate. Cutting back the 337 to run just between Hemel Hempstead and Studham was however a false economy since, despite minimal traffic, there had been some small advantage in the former link to Dunstable. Terminating at Studham created a 'dead leg' operation, and this managed to survive only a little over two years before finally being abandoned completely in July 1973. United Counties provided a replacement service which ran from Luton to Dunstable before covering the old 337 to Hemel Hempstead. Withdrawals and changes such as these began to be made at an increasing pace all across the network over the first two or three years, as London Country tried to cut costs.

From the early 1970s high inflation began to eat away further at operators' margins with significant increases in costs. These could only be countered by fare increases, and so at the beginning of January 1972, service cuts were combined with an increase which saw the basic short distance fares rise by 20%, and middle distance fares by 12%. Over the next three years, as operators everywhere tried to balance inflating costs with fewer passengers, fare increases became ever more frequent, and during 1975/76 London Country's fares increased by more than a third.

After the 723 was converted to omo at the beginning of 1972, Grays used the displaced RCLs to replace its RTs. The 370 was the most important route, requiring 17 buses although RMCs were rostered during the week so that the higher capacity RCLs could be used on the busy local services and many factory journeys. RCL 2245 is running into Romford near the end of its journey from Tilbury. (Capital Transport)

The first new AEC Reliance Green Line coaches – the RPs – arrived at the beginning of 1972, and went into service on the 721 Brentwood to London route. The RCLs which they replaced went mostly to Reigate and Dorking to replace RTs on the 405 and 414, and Romford garage was converted to all-omo. In April the first of the Leyland Atlanteans arrived, followed by more throughout the year. The initial 30 came from a diverted Midland Red order and went to Hertford, Guildford, and Leatherhead to convert important trunk routes to omo. The 408 and 470 had been a joint operation between Guildford, Leatherhead and Chelsham, but conversion of these routes, as they were, proved unworkable. The 408 had one of the longest end-to-end running times of 2hrs 13mins for the full length from Guildford to Chelsham with another seven minutes for journeys which ran on to Warlingham Park or Farleigh, although by 1971 these were confined to Sundays only. Even the shorter 470 was timed at 1hr 51mins from Dorking to Chelsham.

The 409 remained generally busy as far as Godstone, but south of there on the long run to East Grinstead and Forest Row, passengers were often few and far between. Godstone rarely used its RCLs on the route, but after seven years, many of its original batch of RMLs became due for re-certification leading to shortages of available buses. The three RCLs for the 709 were probably the least used buses in the fleet, but they could be employed all day on Saturday if needs be when there was no service on the 709. In 1973 RCL 2237 looks resplendent in full Green Line livery and has stopped at the Crown Inn at Forest Row before running down to the terminus at the old station yard. They were fitted only with these 'lazy' blind displays. (John Bishop)

The 716/716A were among the first routes to be allocated new RPs in April 1972. In Park Lane, RP 65 is working a 716A to Hatfield with RP 53 behind on a 716 to Hitchin, and both coaches seem to be empty. Something – probably a breakdown - has gone badly wrong however since the two coaches should be running 30 minutes apart and the driver of RP 65 seems to be signalling to passengers to board RP 53 behind. (Colin Fradd)

In converting to omo, the running time for the whole length of the 408 would have had to be increased by 15 minutes and this created workings which were too long and would have required longer layovers. The two routes were therefore cut back to West Croydon which permitted workable duties for the drivers, but even this left the remaining Croydon to Guildford section of the 408 with a running time of just under two hours. The new schedules worked such that the total allocations at Chelsham, Leatherhead and Guildford remained unchanged. The new ANs replaced RTs on a one-for-one basis on the 408 and 470, Chelsham's 15 RTs all being retained on the revised 403. Between Croydon and Chelsham the revised 403 timetable replaced the previous joint frequency on the same headway, and between Croydon and Wallington, crew working on the 403 ran jointly with omo on the 408/470. Chelsham's operations became isolated after this change and its crews no longer enjoyed long runs out into the Surrey countryside, being confined instead to the suburbs and heavy traffic through Croydon. But Chelsham's conductors would enjoy another eight years' work as the busy and frequent 403 became the last regular crew operated route, and the last with RTs.

Soon after the RTs were replaced on these major trunk routes, AN 25 and 31 stand in Croydon Bus Station waiting to work their next journeys to Guildford and Dorking. The intermediate blinds on the two buses are slightly different, but both have been set correctly. That on AN 31 was used for the 470, and for 408 journeys as far as Effingham, whereas that on AN 25 was used for the full length of the 408. (John Bishop)

By the end of 1972 Atlanteans had also gone to Garston and Luton to convert the major 321 trunk route, Watford town services and the 803 peak express service between Uxbridge and Welwyn Garden City. Town services at Crawley were converted, and in October the complex Stevenage town services were converted with 17 ANs replacing 19 RTs on the all-day schedules. Stevenage retained only two RTs, left to work the peak hour factory journeys which also included a couple of peak workings to Letchworth on the 384B and to Hitchin on the 303/303C. A previous odd RT working had been a short journey to Aston on the 390 after the morning peak to balance the crew schedule, but this was withdrawn with the October changes. By February 1973, the last of the first batch of 120 ANs had gone to Grays for conversion of most of its crew operated routes. This allowed the majority of RTs to be withdrawn, and in the first three years of London Country's management a total of 392 out of the original 484 had gone. The 90 new RP Reliance Green Line coaches were also in service by this time, completing one-man conversion of what remained of the Green Line network, with the sole exception of the three RCLs kept at Godstone for the 709. The timetable for this had been reduced on Monday to Friday to only three morning and evening peak hour journeys to London, with no service at all on Saturdays and two return Sunday journeys requiring just one coach. To convert the 709 to omo would have meant allocating three new coaches which would have stood idle for the majority of the week and would have been a waste of precious new resources. The saving on the conductors' duties was simply not cost effective when compared to the cost of new coaches, and thus the 709 continued to be crew worked for another four years until enough new single deckers became available. With the new RPs in service, the displaced Routemaster coaches had all been reallocated to bus routes. The newest RCLs were only six years old when these fine vehicles were downgraded, changing circumstances having meant they had never really fulfilled their potential as Green Line coaches.

From about April 1972, the NBC corporate identity began to be imposed across all its subsidiaries. The long distance coach network was branded as 'National Express' and, despite the poor choice of the overall white livery, it brought benefits to the system. The previous countrywide coach route network, operated by all the individual companies, was somewhat disparate and there was a certain lack of co-ordination in many areas. Apart from London's Victoria Coach Station, there were few main interchange facilities, although the 'Associated Motorways' network was a worthy exception with many routes converging on Cheltenham and Birmingham. The major disappointment, perhaps mostly for enthusiasts, was the disappearance of all the former individual and distinctive coach liveries, many of which, such as Royal Blue, Bristol Greyhound, United and Black & White, projected an image of high quality. However the marketing of National Express with its new image, more interchange points and a countrywide route numbering system was a success and coach travel increased.

The great mistake that NBC made however was applying the same process to its bus services. At first, the corporate identity required either the universal red or green fleet colour with no relief whatsoever except by pale grey wheels and fleet numbers with white fleetnames. Even when new, buses looked drab and uninspiring, and the paint itself proved to be of poor quality, soon losing its initial gloss. The imposition of the new corporate image required many existing buses to be repainted, although many former Tilling vehicles (which were all red or green anyway) remained in their traditional Tilling colour with just the addition of the white fleetname. All former liveries soon began to disappear as older buses were replaced by new, and others were repainted. The former Tilling red or green were much more attractive shades than the new NBC colours, but the greatest loss were the individual liveries, mostly of former BET fleets.

The omo conversions with new ANs at Garston did not include the 306 which continued to be crew operated with RMLs, but as their availability became ever more uncertain, the use of RTs became a daily feature. RT 3752 was one of a number which Garston managed to retain and looks in very good condition at Leavesden terminus in July 1975 waiting to work back to Borehamwood. (Ian Pringle)

These two pictures perfectly illustrate the point made in the text about the awful NBC overall leaf green livery when compared with the original LCBS green and yellow. XF 6 has been freshly painted in LCBS livery as it stops to pick up passengers at Red Cross in Reigate on a 424 to East Grinstead, whereas XF 3, is drab and unappealing in NBC livery which looked even worse on double deckers than it did on single deckers. The works journeys on the 438 were cross worked from the 424 allocation, and XF 3 is on its way to Crawley on one of these. (Peter Horner/ Barry Le Jeune)

Southdown's apple green and cream had been somehow synonymous with southern England. East Kent's cherry red and cream with its large gold block capital fleet-names conveyed an air of quality, and colourful fleets like Aldershot & District and City of Oxford were all gradually subsumed into the NBC standard. Aldershot & District were merged with Thames Valley and for a time some of A&D's buses were repainted NBC green before being repainted again into red, which was the chosen colour for the combined Alder Valley fleet. As for London Country, their yellow relief, fleetnames and 'flying polo' logo had resulted in an extremely attractive livery, but this too was soon overtaken by the new corporate identity. It was ironic however that because of the desperate vehicle shortages London Country would suffer, it became impossible to take buses out of service for a repaint so that the green and yellow livery lasted much longer than was intended on much of the fleet.

Apart from the new livery, staff were issued with a new blue/grey uniform with a rather oddly shaped cap, and bus stop flags everywhere were replaced with a new universal version. Whilst the cost of all this is not recorded, a few million pounds and many thousands of man hours were spent repainting buses, supplying uniforms, and driving to every remote corner of the country in small vans to replace what were perfectly functional bus stop flags. This was all done in the completely mistaken belief that bus passengers everywhere would be impressed by the new nationwide corporate image. Advertising campaigns, posters, and the mascot 'Beeper the Frog' all exhorted the public to travel with the slogan *'together we can really go places'*. This was of course complete nonsense and failed to understand that bus passengers are almost entirely local to their area and not remotely interested in such corporate imagery. Given the NBC's parlous financial position at the time, the imposition of all this, even at the time, seemed to be short sighted and a significant waste of precious resources.

In the development of new vehicles, one of the earliest initiatives by the NBC was a joint venture with British Leyland for a standard bus which would become the Leyland National. Seven prototypes had been built in 1970 and in addition to extensive factory testing, had been sent to Spain and Sweden to test them in extreme hot and cold conditions. Given that the NBC regarded the National as the 'all purpose' new generation of single decker, it was however an astonishing omission that none of the prototypes were ever sent to British operators to test in service. A few weeks on arduous city services in all weather conditions would have proved invaluable and given British Leyland much useful feedback on possible faults and weaknesses. The economies of scale which supposedly came from standardisation also resulted in operators being given no choice of engine. A great many operators – especially those within the former Tilling group – wanted the tried and tested Gardner engine, but the Leyland 510 was the only unit offered, a decision which lost the National a number of potential orders.

The first Leyland National for service was delivered to Cumberland on 15th March 1972, closely followed by another to Northern General, and as production increased, large numbers came into service in the second half of 1972. Given the lack of testing in service, it was no surprise that many early faults became apparent. Most of these were minor, but a tendency to catch fire due to overheating engine oil, some fuel leaks, and the ease with which a front wheel skid could occur in wet or icy conditions did not endear the National to fleet engineers or drivers in their early days. The National's fuel consumption at about 8 mpg on average was also about 40% more than many of the buses it was meant to replace, such as the Bristol RE and single deck Daimler Fleetline which commonly returned better than 12 mpg.

They were therefore not well received at first, but it was at least a generally well thought-out design with a number of technical innovations. Despite the initial reservations, the National went on to become a reliable and durable bus, many putting in long service lives. It was however, 'built down to a budget' and although some aspects were improved over the years, and the Gardner engine was offered later, it always seemed to suffer – perhaps unfairly – from a perception of being 'cheap and basic'. It is true that the quality of vehicles produced throughout much of the 1970s by British Leyland was at best average and often appalling, and this did nothing for the Leyland National's early years.

Drivers who had always used engine noise to help judge gear changes were beginning to get used to rear engined buses where engine noise was less audible,

SNB 273 illustrates the National Bus Company standard corporate livery as it pulls away from the stop in Dartford Market Street on one of the few remaining 423 peak hour journeys to Wrotham. Swanley received new Nationals in July 1977 to convert the 423 to omo, its SMs mostly being transferred to Dartford for more omo conversions there. Despite their early teething problems and basic interiors, they proved to be reliable and gave good service. (Colin Fradd)

and the power steering with the main weight behind the rear axles gave the bus a very light feel. A Hertford driver told me soon after their introduction that he thought the National was 'a good modern bus' but he had found them difficult to get used to, especially with a good load at speed, and that they could be unpredictable on wet roads.

London Country's dire need for omo single deckers meant that very few RFs could be withdrawn in the early years, but as the influx of new double deckers continued, the Leyland National offered an opportunity to begin replacing RFs on many routes. London Country's first examples were dual door long versions, four of which were first delivered direct to Nottingham for use on an experimental City centre shopping route. I travelled on LN 8 and LN 11 on 10th March 1973 in Nottingham, and it was my first experience of them. The initial impression was just how different the bus was from everything else at the time, but what was most noticeable was the spartan interior and the high level of interior noise from the engine. The noisy engines, whether inside or out, became one of the National's less endearing features, and standing near one as it pulled away sometimes came close to the need for ear plugs!

The 431 had been converted to omo RF at the end of 1966 and was one of the first routes to be part converted to LNBs. It included a long steep climb up Star Hill from Dunton Green to Knockholt Pound, and RF 169 appears to be empty as it begins the ascent on a journey to Orpington. Dunton Green was its last garage and it was finally withdrawn in June 1975 in its 24th year, being sold for scrap a few months later. (Colin Fradd)

London Country's first few Nationals went to Stevenage at the end of 1972 for use on the 'SuperBus' town services. These routes became a testing ground for some SMs and Metro Scanias alongside the Nationals, and with their eye-catching blue and yellow livery with large 'SB' logos, this network became a great success in contrast to the continuing decline almost everywhere else.

At the very beginning of 1973, the first Leyland Nationals for conventional bus routes went to Dunton Green where they were principally intended for the 493 Orpington Town service. These were long LNBs, and the operational problem with this was that buses worked positioning journeys on either the 431 or 471 from Sevenoaks or Dunton Green to Orpington to take up service on the 493, and the combined schedules also meant that other 431/471 journeys were worked by these long Nationals. Except for a short section of narrow lane from Well Hill to Chelsfield the 431 route was generally wide enough, but this was certainly not the case on the 471. The road from Scotts Lodge through Cudham down to Green Street Green was narrow all the way, and even in the days of GS operation there were many places where a GS could not pass a car coming the other way, let alone anything bigger. The LNBs were about 50% longer than a GS with a much longer wheelbase, and with their bigger mirrors were at least a foot wider. They were far too big for a route like the 471, and the run through Cudham was something of a lottery for the driver. One Saturday afternoon in June 1973 I travelled on LNB 22 from Sevenoaks to Orpington on the 471 and the bus got stuck three times along this narrow lane to the extent that almost ten minutes were lost by the time Green Street Green was reached. The driver, an elderly man who had almost certainly spent many years driving GSs down Cudham Lane, was the model of patience, but was less than complimentary about the huge vehicle he was expected to thread along narrow lanes with high banks and hedges on both sides! Another batch of these early long Nationals went to Hatfield for town services in February 1973, and then a little later several more to convert the trunk 303/303A which were much more suited to this arduous route. Despite their drab all-over leaf green NBC livery, they looked quite impressive, and relieved some MBs which had run the route for a short time out of necessity to replace the hapless SMs mentioned earlier.

The Stevenage Superbus routes came from the success of the Blue Arrow service begun by London Transport three days before London Country took over. In March 1971 the Blue Arrow route to Chells was altered, and in July the Superbus network began with the SB1 to Chells, followed in September by the SB2 to St Nicholas. London Country purchased four of these Metro-Scanias specifically for the SB routes, and in 1973 acquired three more from Hants & Dorset in exchange for three LNBs. On 16th August 1971, MS 2 waits in Stevenage bus station on the Chells service. Being completely non-standard to the main fleet, the spares shortages rendered them more difficult to keep running and they were all withdrawn during 1978.
(Alan Charman)

In February 1973, Hatfield was the second garage to receive LNBs for town services around Hatfield and Welwyn Garden City. LNB 14 is working a 340A journey, the route number blind illustrating the problem where routes had suffix letters which could not be accommodated on the standard three track blinds and had to be included in the destination display. Suffix letters were gradually withdrawn either by incorporating them into the main route number, or by a new route number altogether. The LNs' excessive length – 37 feet – and long front and rear overhangs gave rise to difficulties on some routes and they were not a success, having a relatively short life with London Country. During 1979, when only six years old, it was decided not to overhaul them and most were soon sold. (Capital Transport)

At the same time as the first long Nationals went onto bus routes, others arrived for Green Line service and I clearly recall the first sight of one of these. With their half green and half white 'local coach' National livery with green 'Green Line' fleetnames on the roof cove panels, they looked quite smart and impressive from the outside. Inside though, they were truly dreadful. The seats were brown plastic with thin cushions, passengers in the front lower floor section could barely see out of the windows, and in no time at all the blown air ventilation left pattern stains on the ceiling cove panels. Leg room was not generous even for an average person, and the heating system seemed to be either 'hot' or 'cold' with nothing in between. The external paint was of poor quality and soon deteriorated, losing its early shine, and bus washing machines soon began to wear away the fleetname transfers. A journey on one of these was like sitting in a 'sounding box' in what seemed like a cavernous interior where the engine noise was all-consuming. London Country soon changed policy and ordered the short version, but these were just as bad as the longer ones, though British Leyland did start to fit moquette to the seats instead of the dreadful PVC. In winter they were

The 721 was the first route to receive RPs in January 1972, but only 13 months later they were replaced with some of the first LNCs. Whist they looked impressive externally, the interiors were appalling and undoubtedly hastened the decline of the 721, although they did not survive at Romford long enough to see the withdrawal of the route in July 1977. LNC 31 is running through the east London suburbs to Aldgate and was one of those soon demoted to bus routes. Few survived the first expiry of their CoFs. (Capital Transport)

often cold, and a Green Line journey of any length was not a pleasant experience. I can still clearly recall an early morning journey on the 727 from Uxbridge to Luton on LNC 55 a few days before Christmas 1974. It was a bitterly cold morning, the bus was 35 minutes late, and the inside was little warmer than outside. The noise, the cold, and the thin plastic seats completed what was perhaps one of the least comfortable journeys ever taken, and summed up just how far the once grand Green Line network had sunk. Nobody knows how many more passengers were driven away as a result of their introduction.

Leyland had promised an upgraded 'semi coach' version of the National, but London Country's need for new vehicles was so urgent they could not wait for them and did not receive any until August 1974, by which time the 706, 708, 711, 712, 713, 714, 719, 721, 724 and 727 had all been completely or mostly converted with either the long or short version of these buses. On the 706, Chelsham managed to retain its RFs because the long Leyland Nationals were physically too big for the garage. The 706 rosters meant that drivers drove only buses from their own garage, but there were exceptions on some of the peak workings to Westerham and on Sundays, when Chelsham's drivers had to take over a Tring based LNC. One can but guess at their thoughts! Whether, with hindsight, less damage would have been done by retaining the remaining RFs until the semi-coach Nationals became available is pure speculation, but in any event the RFs were 20 years old with many becoming due for re-certification and so had to be replaced. When the first of the semi-coach Nationals did arrive, they went at least some way to improving comfort with their moquette covered high backed seats, deeper cushions and overhead luggage racks. The first batch went to Grays in August 1974 allowing the ill-fated RC Reliances to be withdrawn at last from Green Liine service, the whole batch being sent to Hertford to replace some of the 23 RFs still rostered there. In September 1974 the 701/702 were converted to new semi-coach Nationals so that, apart from Chelsham's RFs on the 706, all scheduled Green Line RFs had finally been replaced. After this, the remaining dual-purpose Nationals went to replace some of the long 'bus' versions, but by the end of 1974 there were still 51 'bus version' SNC/LNC vehicles rostered for Green Line work.

After an unsatisfactory period on the 711, the hapless RCs were repainted and sent to Grays at the beginning of 1972 to convert the 723 to omo, allowing the displaced RCLs to replace RTs on Grays local routes. This was probably the least demanding Green Line route and they performed reasonably well until they were demoted to bus work and sent to Hertford in August 1974. RC 6 displays the NBC 'local coach' livery as it heads through Belhus on a journey back to Grays. (Colin Fradd)

The 'country' section of the 318 between Croxley and Hemel Hempstead was another route ideal for omo, but was not converted until July 1973, when it was renumbered 352. It was nominally rostered for operation with MBs with a handful of RF journeys, but the use of RFs became more frequent as Garston's vehicle shortages worsened. On a bright spring day, RF 550 pauses at Sarratt Green on a journey back to Watford. (Ian Pringle)

Having been sent to Hertford, the RCs lasted another three years meandering along Hertfordshire's country lanes or on busier routes. They were not well received, especially by Hertford's engineering staff, but their troublesome reputation was at least less of a problem than on front line Green Line work. By the time the last ones went from Hertford in January 1977, they were less than 12 years old, having remained unpopular with both drivers and engineering staff to the end. They had replaced RFs when they arrived in 1965, and the great irony was that when they departed, Hertford had one last RF still in service.

Despite the influx of new Nationals and Reliances however, events would soon show that regular RF workings on Green Line routes were far from over. Their reliability and rugged performance saw them replacing failed new buses time and again, and they were still preferred by the majority of drivers given the opportunity. On a 704 journey from Victoria to Slough one Sunday evening in July 1972, RF 267 appeared instead of the scheduled RP. The driver was running almost 20 minutes late at Victoria due to heavy traffic, but after Hammersmith it cleared, and with few stops the RF was really put through its paces, arriving at Slough almost on time having caught up the deficit. The driver told me that when he had signed on at Windsor garage at lunchtime that day, he was supposed to have taken out the scheduled RP, but saw the RF standing in the garage, so quickly swapped over the running number plates from the RP and took the RF instead. In the previous week he'd suffered two breakdowns with RPs, and when running late he said it was far more difficult to catch up time again with an RP than with an RF. He and some of his fellow drivers were glad that Windsor had a few remaining RFs since they could still be relied upon to run all day.

After the Green Line Leyland Nationals had arrived, the standard bus version was purchased in large numbers to the extent that eventually London Country built up the largest fleet among all the NBC companies. In April 1973 there were around 115 RFs still scheduled for operation on the less frequent rural routes, although this is far from precise since interworking between routes had increased greatly as timetables were cut and omo extended. Whilst withdrawals and more cuts reduced this number during the year there was still a need for a smaller more manoeuvrable single decker to operate along lanes where the Leyland National was less practical. The bus chosen was the short version of the Bristol LH which had been introduced in 1967 to replace the successful MW, and the SU which, although built in smaller numbers than the MW, had also proved a useful small capacity bus for rural work. The LH would become a National Bus Company standard with varying chassis combinations and bodies from the small basic 30-seat bus to the longer luxury coach version and was very successful. By the time production finished in 1981 a total of 1,218 LH variants had been built, the vast majority of which were the standard LH bus chassis. London Transport decided on the 30ft long standard bus with semi-automatic gearchange, which was an almost direct replacement for the RF in terms of size but with a greater seating capacity. London Country however decided on the short LHS version, which despite its shorter length, still had a seating capacity of 35 albeit with rather less legroom than an RF. It was however only available with manual transmission, and since the number of drivers who had once worked on GSs or still had manual licences was rapidly declining, large numbers of drivers had to be trained and tested before they could drive the LHS, the process taking three months before sufficient drivers were available to allow them to come into service. The first ones arrived in June 1973 at St Albans and Dunton Green, followed by Amersham in December, and had standard 8ft wide bodies, 6ins wider than the RFs they replaced. The first batch consisted of only 23 buses, but the next 30 were built to the narrower 7ft 6ins wide version since there were sections of some routes which were felt to be too narrow for anything wider. This was a curious idiosyncrasy of London Country who specified narrower bodies where the vast majority of their NBC contemporaries and Tilling predecessors had run 8ft wide buses along the narrowest of lanes quite successfully for many years, especially so given the width of the Leyland Nationals then coming into service. The LHS was a good solid and functional bus, but its great drawback was the poor ride quality along rough roads. Its short wheelbase in relation to the overall length caused the bus to 'buck' up and down to the extent that a tight grip was necessary to avoid being bounced up and down too much, especially if seated at the back. The second batch of 30 were all in service by the end of 1974, being spread widely across many garages to replace RFs, mostly on rural routes. Having purchased 53 LHSs, it was another three years before a final batch of 14 more were delivered. There had been no intention to purchase a second small batch, but they became spare as other companies reduced or cancelled orders in the face of continuing service reductions. London Country therefore took advantage of the situation, but by 1977 when they went into service there was limited need for them in terms of allocations. However, such was the shortage of serviceable buses that they were distributed around the fleet and often used as substitutes as much as for formal allocation, some even finding their way onto the odd Green Line working.

After four years, the large influx of new buses had allowed significant progress towards the ultimate goal of 100% one-man operation. Service reductions and the

The 377 was a Hemel Hempstead works service linking Apsley Mills and factories to the north including the Brocks firework factory at Cupid Green. The main service to Redbourn was provided by the hourly 307, but the 377 had a couple of peak hour journeys extended there, and in May 1973, RT 611 is about to turn right opposite Two Waters garage towards the town centre on one of these workings. Shortly after this, the Redbourn journeys were withdrawn among many timetable cuts to local services. (Capital Transport)

In 1974 BL 19 climbs up Chartridge Lane away from Chesham on a 348 circular journey via Lee Common and Hyde Heath back to Chesham. The 348 circular working had been introduced in 1972, replacing part of the 359. The rural routes from Chesham suffered a dramatic loss of passengers and went through probably more changes than anywhere else, sections of routes 348, 359, 394 and 397 being interchanged several times. In November 1975, this circular service was abandoned as part of the severe cuts referred to in the text. (Colin Fradd)

RF 26 was the first Green Line coach delivered in October 1951 and one of the first to be modernised in 1966. Less than two years later however it was downgraded to bus status and went to Dorking where it spent several years. It has stopped outside the White Hart in Dorking High Street looking shabby with a mix of two shades of green and the white NBC waistband. In 1975 it was transferred to Crawley where it was finally withdrawn at the end of that year. It was later preserved and restored to its 1966 condition, and for a time operated by Memory Lane on their Dorking to Guildford Sunday service, on which route the author was fortunate enough to drive it on several occasions. (Colin Fradd)

withdrawal of loss-making services had reduced the fleet size, and local authorities were beginning to get to grips with more co-ordinated funding of those routes requiring subsidy. London Country was still some way from turning a profit, but the dire situation inherited in 1970 had at least been arrested. At the start of 1974, the total Monday to Friday peak scheduled run-out compared to January 1970 had been reduced from 1,122 to 999, from 856 to 773 on Saturdays and from 389 to 345 on Sundays. More significant was that, whereas 646 out of the 1,122 scheduled for service on 1st January 1970 were crew operated, the figure had been reduced to only 250 out of the 999 at the start of 1974. On Sundays the 164 crew buses scheduled on 1st January 1970 had been reduced to just 19. The Green Line routes had all been completely converted, but the major savings in conductors had come from a wholesale conversion of crew worked routes which, by 1974, included many of the main trunk routes.

In Surrey, the 425 and 439 routes were rationalised in July 1973. The 425 was extended from Dorking to Redhill over the 439 routeing through Brockham and Leigh, with the 439 itself retaining the circular Newdigate routeing and extended over the 425 to Guildford. This was a novel revision which saved a bus but retained the basic service levels largely unaltered, even including the hourly Sunday headway to Guildford through the day until late evening. The Guildford to Dorking and Brockham sections retained reasonable loads, but this was not the case over the rest of the two routes. Although the evening service into Redhill was withdrawn, retaining the two-hourly headway through Leigh seemed ambitious, and beyond Strood Green through Parkgate and Newdigate back to the main road at Beare Green, traffic potential – apart from Newdigate itself – had all but disappeared. There may still have been the odd person from Newdigate who worked in Dorking, but there were minimal shoppers, and three or four shopping journeys during the day would probably have been quite sufficient. But the new timetable maintained the two-hourly headway in both directions round this circular part of the 439, so that on Saturdays there were still 14 journeys to and from Dorking which was far too many, and only four fewer than five years earlier when London Transport was beginning to prune the timetable. Given the necessity for service reductions, maintaining this seemed at odds with all the other cuts made during 1973. What was cut though was the service between Dorking and Westcott where almost all of the short journeys had gone, reducing the Saturday service to 43 journeys in total. Fifteen years earlier, the Dorking to Westcott section had enjoyed 94 journeys on Saturdays, Dorking allocating an RF all day just to work these short journeys, so that by July 1973 the service along this once busy part had been cut by more than half.

Tillingbourne, continued to suffer losses and unreliability, and tried to counter London Country's revised 425/439 service by changing their own timetables between Gomshall, Albury and Guildford to run just ahead of London Country who complained formally to the Traffic Commissioners. London Country's drivers reported that Tillingbourne drivers were deliberately running late on some journeys so they could run just in front of the London Country service in an attempt to abstract traffic. After a few months and a meeting to clear the air, Tillingbourne changed the 450 timetable between Albury and Guildford in January 1974 to give a more even headway over the common section. So severe though were Tillingbourne's financial and operational difficulties (the lease on their premises had expired) that in early 1974, they offered the business to London Country who – understandably – were unable to offer sufficient and did not proceed. It was therefore ironic that a decade later, Tillingbourne should have recovered sufficiently that they eventually took over the 412, 425 and 439 from London Country in fundamental changes which would in the end lead to the closure of Dorking garage.

By the end of 1973, the steady programme of service cuts and withdrawals had

Dorking garage was allocated two new BNs in September 1974 to replace two RFs. Interworking saw them used on all routes, and on a frosty winter day BN 34 has turned at Strood Green, Brockham, working one of the short journeys through Dorking to Westcott which were still then a feature of the 425/439 timetable, but which would be drastically cut back over the next few years. (Colin Fradd).

accelerated, 15 mostly rural routes having been completely withdrawn with sections of many others abandoned. These included the 359 between Great Missenden and Aylesbury, 336 on Saturdays between Rickmansworth and Watford, 413 from Ide Hill to Brasted, 421 beyond Kemsing to Heverham, the handful of journeys on the 333 to the tiny hamlet of Chapmore End, the 364 Luton to Hitchin and many others. Those rural routes which had survived suffered considerable cuts with timetables reduced to just a few worthwhile journeys. The Saturday service into Berkhamsted on the 317 which had once enjoyed nine journeys plus another five on the 352 had been cut to just three in the morning only with the last bus back from Berkhamsted at 12.37pm. The once hourly 350 to Potters Bar had just five journeys left with the section down to New Barnet withdrawn completely, while the Sunday service consisted of only three afternoon/ evening journeys between Hertford and Bishops Stortford. The weekday through service from Hitchin to St Albans during shopping hours on the 304 had been reduced to two departures from Hitchin at 9.46am and 3.37pm with just a short to Whitwell at 12.46pm in between, plus one additional departure on Tuesdays and Fridays for market day. The 462 which once had a 30-minute headway had been reduced to every two hours beyond Fetcham all the way to Chertsey. Evening services on rural routes were almost non-existent, and almost 90 routes had no Sunday service at all, perhaps one of the most important being the 301/302 from Watford to Hemel Hempstead and Aylesbury. In the heyday of the late 1950s where 11 RTs had been required all day on Sunday for these routes, by 1974, all that remained was a single RF to work just one early morning journey to Watford and back, the rest of the road being left to the 706/708 Green Line service, and even this was halved when the 706 was withdrawn in April 1977. All over the network, where 30-minute Saturday headways had survived on what busy routes remained, the majority were reduced to hourly.

Although a minor route, the 421 had remained crew worked mainly due to some occasional heavy loads from Kemsing. It was converted to omo in January 1972, the section beyond Kemsing to Heverham being abandoned at the same time. Later that year, RF 586 has stopped at Otford Pond on a journey back to Sevenoaks with an unidentified SM on a 401 towards Dartford in the background. (Colin Fradd)

When SNBs converted the 301 and 302 to omo in May 1975, RTs had previously run the route continuously for 27 years. RT 3117 spent two years on the routes before conversion, but like many of Hemel Hempstead's RTs went for further service at Garston to cover their shortage of RMLs. In Hemel Hempstead bus station, it waits to pull on to the stand for a journey to Little Bushey. The coach in the background was acquired from the failed Court Line operation by United Counties and is on the route to Dunstable which had replaced London Country's 337. (Ian Pringle)

On a wet day, a filthy RF 559 has arrived at Iver Heath on a short 452 working from Windsor which was run as a positioning journey to get the bus to Iver for the afternoon duty on the 459. This consisted of four return trips between Richings Park and Uxbridge, after which the bus worked to Iver before running as a 458 back to Windsor. By the time this picture was taken in 1975, the 459 had become almost pointless and would be finally abandoned the following year. The bus was one of a small number repainted into full NBC livery, but would be withdrawn at the end of 1975. (Colin Fradd)

Since the end of the 1960s, manufacturers had struggled to keep up with demand for new buses with many orders being delivered well beyond promised dates. Demand had peaked as large numbers of buses delivered in the immediate post-war years all came up for replacement within a few short years, and the slow delivery of new buses had delayed many operators' replacement programmes, few more than London Country whose need for so many new buses had been paramount. By 1974, whilst deliveries were beginning to catch up, the capacity to supply sufficient spare parts fell behind and shortages began to develop. At the beginning of 1974, in addition to its new buses, London Country also had a total of around 460 RTs, RFs and Routemasters, which were reliant on London Transport for

spare parts and who had to give priority to its own fleet when spares were required. As large numbers of London Country's ex-LTE buses came due for re-certification, without enough spares for even routine running repairs, increasing numbers had to be taken out of service. The nationwide shortage of spares was a poor reflection on manufacturers, badly affecting all operators, and for London Country a situation rapidly developed to the point where the number of buses actually available for service fell increasingly below the daily scheduled totals. During 1974, 33 withdrawn RFs were recertified for service as enough spares became available, but as can be seen from the table below, this was by no means enough to ease the shortages. The situation worsened throughout 1974, with around 350 vehicles delicensed by the autumn, including four out of ten SMs and about one third of the RPs. Whilst the situation changed daily, it could not be improved, and the table for August 1975 shows how impossible the situation had become.

TOTAL STOCK AND AVAILABILITY AT 31st AUGUST 1975

Type	Total owned	Total not serviceable	Withdrawn or in store	Total available	Total scheduled for service	Total trainers scheduled	Shortfall	Surplus
RT	88	24	12	52	33	15		4
RMC	69	17	3	49	60		11	
RCL	43	8		35	39		4	
RML	97	45		52	90		38	
XF	8	1		7	7			
AF	11	1		10	10			
AN	123	5	1	117	110			7
RF	166	40	47	79	80		1	
RC	13	5		8	11		3	
RP	90	16	1	73	78		5	
MB	32	8		24	25		1	
MBS	76	20	1	55	67		12	
SM	138	38	2	98	125		27	
SMA	21	6	1	14	18		4	
SMW	15	5	1	9	14		5	
BL / BN	53	4		49	47			2
LN /LNB	43	2		41	40			1
LNC	24	2		22	21			1
SNB	36	1		35	34			1
SNC	71	1	1	69	60			9
LS	3			3	3			
TOTALS	1220	249	70	901	972	15	-111	25
% of TOTAL		20.41	5.74	73.85				

SOURCE:- LOTS SUP 5 Allocations at 31st August 1975

The 319 had four suffix numbers and many variations for odd works and schoolday journeys, two of which are illustrated here. RF 611 is working one of the two 319D school journeys to Langleybury school near Kings Langley and was one of those repainted in the appalling overall NBC leaf green. It ended its days at Amersham before withdrawal in August 1975. RF 168 looks very shabby in May 1976 as it runs back to Two Waters garage on the single 319C lunchtime journey to the Ovaltine factory at Kings Langley. Soon after this it went for a few months to St Albans, then to Garston where it was withdrawn in November the following year. (Ian Pringle)

The Routemaster fleet was the worst affected with one in three off the road. Not only were the SMs less reliable than other newer types, but the spares shortages also resulted in one in five of them being unavailable, which, given that they were all less than five years old, was a scandalous position. The position with the equally new RPs and was just as bad – only 73 out of 90 being available for service. The number of Leyland Nationals and Atlanteans coming into service was increasing all the time, and despite some of their shortcomings, they at least – together with the Bristol LHs – were more reliable.

The table shows that overall one-fifth of the entire fleet was unserviceable, with the net result that the Monday to Friday peak scheduled requirement was short of 86 buses, not allowing for the normal engineering spares which increased the daily operational shortage even more. Although the actual total varied from day to day, cancellation of numerous individual journeys was unavoidable on a daily basis, and some garages were forced to cancel specific journeys on a permanent basis while the crisis continued. Further numbers of RTs and RFs were re-certified where possible to cover other vehicles, and RFs in particular could be seen covering almost anything, particularly for SMs and on a number of Green Line duties. The daily position also varied greatly from garage to garage, with those relying on numbers of Routemasters being worst affected. Garston was in the worst position with only six of its 23 RMLs available. The maximum scheduled was 21, so it was 15 short, and even the 12 serviceable RTs it had were still not enough for the daily run out. Eight of its 22 MB/MBS fleet were also unavailable, but as the requirement was for 13, there was one spare in theory, so it was not uncommon for this to be turned out to cover a double deck duty. At Windsor, 50% of the 18 RMLs there were unserviceable, leaving it seven short for service with only two RTs and a lone RMC to help out. Northfleet had 22 RMLs to cover 20 duties, but nine were unserviceable, and it had no RTs. Northfleet and Dartford needed ten SMA for their joint share of the 725, but had only six available between them, so the spare RFs which Dartford had became a common sight on the 725. Staines had a smaller allocation of RMLs, but with only five of its eight serviceable it did not have enough to run its share of the 441 and, although there was one spare RT, it could not borrow anything from nearby Windsor which was even worse off. Addlestone had the largest allocation of SMs with 27, nine of which were unserviceable leaving them four short for daily service, but four RFs just made up the shortfall. Eight out of 15 SMs at Swanley were unserviceable, but since all 15 were scheduled, they were in an impossible position. There were four spare RFs, but this still left them three short, although a spare SNC could be used during the week as the 719 needed the extra coach only on Sundays. This was still insufficient and nearby Dartford had no spares, so cancellations on the busy 423 were unavoidable, although they managed to just about run the 477 since they had just enough serviceable RMCs.

Reigate's RTs for the 414 were replaced by RCLs early in 1972, a few RMCs coming later for other routes. Before long however, the inability to keep Routemasters running meant that any type available was used. RMC 1479 is working a through 414 journey to Horsham and is about to turn off the main Redhill/Reigate road into Blackborough Road and down to the bus garage. As was often the case correct blinds were in short supply, so a set of RT rear intermediate blinds has been fitted. (Peter Plummer)

School journeys also provided a number of odd crew workings and Garston operated some on the 346D from Carpenders Park and Oxhey Estate to two schools in Garston and required three buses morning and afternoon. The RML journeys were worked off the 347 rosters, and the MB journeys from the 318/318A. RML 2318 is working the 4.10pm afternoon return from St Michaels School, and MBS 74 the 4.08pm from Queens School. In 1975, Garston did not have enough serviceable MBs, a number of red ones being hired from London Transport. Garston's RML fleet became so depleted that they frequently ran RML workings with a conductor on a single decker. (Colin Fradd)

St Albans and Hatfield jointly ran the very busy 330 and 341 which required 15 RMC plus two more for odd peak journeys. They had only 11 serviceable buses between them and cancellations were frequent. Les Bland – a St Albans conductor – recalls several duties on the 330 on an MBS which, with few grabrails in the front standee section, was often hazardous for a conductor. Of all the garages operating numbers of Routemasters, only Godstone had enough for service plus a couple of spares, although one of these was loaned almost permanently to East Grinstead whose single RML for the 409 was off the road. This is just a small snapshot of the daily problems and if this was not serious enough, there was also a daily cost in moving what serviceable vehicles there were around the network from garage to garage to fill gaps, even if only for a few days, in a desperate effort to run as much of the schedules as possible.

All of this added significantly to daily running costs, and there was little alternative to increasing fares. Even in a period where high inflation was causing problems in the economy as a whole, the 66% average fare rise which London Country pushed through in 1975 was exceptional, but despite the obvious loss of further passengers resulting from such a huge increase, no other option was really available.

With no immediate prospect of the supply of spares improving, and no prospect of catching up the backlog, hiring buses from other operators was the only alternative available to maintain services. The hiring of a variety of buses from other operators is well recorded, and certainly provided interest for enthusiasts. Some, like the Daimler Roadliners and Fleetlines hired from Bournemouth, proved little more reliable than the buses they were supposed to replace. The Royal Blue Bristol MW Coaches which went to Dunton Green and the Southend Leyland PD3s at Harlow proved to be the most reliable. From an enthusiast's point of view, the Southend buses were by far the most interesting, and they were already 11 years old when they arrived at Harlow in March 1976. With their constant mesh manual gearboxes and distinctive Leyland engine sound, they harked back to the RTLs and RTWs and were a delight to ride on. In 1975, Harlow's Routemasters had all been dispersed elsewhere to assist other less fortunate garages. They had been replaced with 10 RTs, but early in 1976 these also had to be sent to cover for unserviceable Routemasters elsewhere. The Southend buses replaced all the RTs and were used on all of Harlow's routes in the ten months they were there, including the odd turn on the 720 Green Line, although Harlow's drivers were less impressed with the manual gearchange and the slower acceleration when

The 339 was Harlow's last major RT route, due mainly to the fact that the road south from Ongar was less suitable for RMLs with some width restrictions. RTs therefore maintained the route until March 1976 when the Southend PD3s allowed them to be deployed elsewhere. RT 964 however was not redeployed, but withdrawn late in 1975 before being stored at Grays. Here it comes up the hill from Epping Station on a journey to Warley, and Southend 341 near the same spot is on a short journey to Ongar. RML blinds fitted the boxes on the PDs although canopy route numbers had to be used. Note the garage code and running number holders fixed to these buses which London Transport had fitted when they were used from Croydon garage before their transfer to London Country. (Colin Fradd)

compared to the faithful RT. Dartford also had a batch of six PD2s from Maidstone Corporation, which with three Eastbourne Corporation AEC Regents that went to Swanley allowed most of the 423 and 477 schedules to be worked. The Royal Blue MW coaches at Dunton Green had manual hinged doors, couldn't take ticket machines, and so had to be crew operated, but although the garage had become 100% omo in March 1972, working practices had resulted in a number of conductors remaining on the staff. Most had been loaned to Northfleet and Dartford which suffered perennial staff shortages, so the allocation of the Royal Blue coaches to Dunton Green made sense but added considerable running costs to the daily operation. Like the Southend and Maidstone buses, they had manual gearboxes, but plenty of power with their Gardner 6-cylinder engines and provided great comfort with their coach seats. Apart from a number of London Transport red MBs which were sent to various garages (particularly Garston) hired vehicles went to seven garages between October 1975 and March 1978, some staying a few months with the Bournemouth Fleetlines at Leatherhead being amongst the first to arrive and last to leave. At the maximum there were as many as 50 on hire from various operators, and they undoubtedly saved the day at a time when vehicle availability was at its worst.

In addition to hiring buses, London Country had at one point also considered purchasing a number of second hand Leyland PD3s from Southdown with their distinctive 'Queen Mary' full front bodies. They would have replaced Routemasters given that so many of these were unavailable, and the first one arrived at Reigate in March 1975. In the event, only three were purchased and were sent to Godstone a few months later. Retaining their traditional Southdown apple green and cream livery, they looked attractive, but were never more than a temporary solution, being sold on little more than a year later.

Hertfordshire's proactive approach to rural bus routes did result in some small improvements. When the 329 (Hertford – Knebworth – Nup End) had been withdrawn in August 1971 there had been considerable public protest, and so on 31st May 1975 a new route numbered 379 was started between Hertford and Stevenage, resurrecting a service through Bramfield, Bulls Green and Datchworth. The old 329 had been an outstanding example of London Transport's lack of initiative to review the old established route network, the route to Knebworth and Nup End being effectively a 'dead leg' with next to no passengers, and serving only as a link into Hertford. As Stevenage expanded it became an increasingly important destination for people living along the 329, and by the early 1960s, there was an obvious case for diverting the route to Stevenage, while perhaps retaining a limited service from Nup End. London Transport however had done nothing other than cut the 329 timetable steadily back as passengers declined without ever looking at the route itself. The new 379 ran two journeys Tuesday and Friday and three Saturdays, was an immediate success and continued to be well patronised, London Country continuing to run it until it was lost under the new tendering regime in 1988. In a less successful initiative, three Saturday afternoon journeys were reinstated on the 317 into Berkhamsted, giving a two-hourly headway plus a late departure from Hemel Hempstead to Gaddesden. One Sunday afternoon return journey which gave two or three hours for people who wished to visit Ashridge Common was also added. This was soon abandoned as was the late Saturday journey, but the Saturday afternoon service into Berkhamsted proved to be sufficiently successful to justify its continuation. The 317A via Nettleden, which was first intended to be withdrawn after the 1958 strike, remained with just a single journey Monday to Saturday into Hemel Hempstead and back for morning shoppers.

But these small additions did nothing to alter the dire situation which prevailed across the whole of Hertfordshire. Vehicle shortages and continuing losses in the northern area prompted London Country to write to Hertfordshire County Council at the end of 1975 to summarize the situation. They warned for example that it would be necessary to withdraw the remaining 350 timetable to Potters Bar, drastically cut the 308 Saturday service to Cuffley, and completely withdraw the 382 (St Albans – Codicote), 383 (Hitchin – Weston), 384A (Hertford – Great Munden) and 387 (Tring – Aldbury), the last of which would have withdrawn the link from Tring to the railway station which was about 1½ miles outside the town. These were just some of the rural cuts contemplated, but even important routes such as the 301 and 310 trunk routes and some town services were among those causing concern. Of the northern Green Line routes, the 716/716A Green Line were incurring heavy losses. London Country proposed large cuts for the early part of 1976 which would have taken buses out of the schedules at Hemel Hempstead, Garston, Hertford and Stevenage. It was to Hertfordshire's credit that their realistic approach together with London Country's co-operation avoided

The purchase of three Leyland PD3s from Southdown in July 1975 with their distinctive 'Queen Mary' style bodies was odd to say the least. A tentative plan to buy several was not pursued, and the three which were sent to Godstone lasted only 14 months before being sold on. LS 3 has just left West Croydon bus station on a journey to Godstone on the 409 which involved a number of long hills and several gear changes which made them unpopular with Godstone drivers. They could also suffer from brake fade on long descents, and the steep drop down Church Hill in Caterham had to be done slowly in 2nd gear. (Colin Brown)

The six Bristol MW coaches hired from Royal Blue in 1975 provided both comfort and power on the hilly roads in north Kent. Dunton Green used them on almost every route. Most of the 402 was worked by these coaches and fleet number 1437 dating from 1967 is leaving Sevenoaks on a journey to Bromley North. They had to be crew operated and the conductor is next to the driver intent on adjusting something. The SMs they replaced when they arrived would never return to Dunton Green. (Mike Harris)

The last bus to Great Munden. After Dane End, the 384A ran along three miles of single track lane to Great Munden. It had only ever been a minimal service with two journeys during the week and four on Saturdays, and these were gradually reduced until only two journeys remained on Saturday afternoon. At the end of 1975, London Country gave notice that the service would have to be withdrawn, and Hertfordshire were unable to subsidise it any longer. The last day was 3rd May 1976, and BN 49 reverses at the cross roads at the end of the village having worked the 5.45pm from Hertford – the last ever journey. Two teenage girls had alighted in the village and asked the driver when the next bus back to Hertford left. They had some difficulty understanding that this was the last ever bus! (Author)

many of these reductions, although the 382 and 384A would in the end be withdrawn and the 383 taken over by United Counties. One small cut which went largely unnoticed in May 1975 was the end of the through service on 386 from Bishops Stortford to Hitchin. After 1958, through journeys had only run on Saturdays, but these required two buses being out all day on this remote route carrying few passengers. The Saturday service was therefore altered to run as two separate routes from Hertford to either Bishops Stortford or Hitchin in the same way as the Tuesday and Thursday service had been run since 1965. On Tuesdays, the 379 and 386 journeys were interworked, and the same arrangement on Saturdays made better use of the bus while the Bishops Stortford service was cut back, allowing better use of the bus by interworking it on other routes from Hertford rather than it sitting idle at Bishops Stortford during long layovers between shopping journeys.

In Buckinghamshire, it was necessary to make further significant cuts to the network of rural services radiating out from Chesham and Amersham. The time-tables had already been drastically reduced over the previous five years, London Transport also having made some reductions themselves in 1969 before London Country took over. In November 1975 however, timetables were reduced to little more than skeleton shopping and schools journeys. The route to Tring was left with only six journeys Monday to Friday and four Saturdays. There were two or three extra journeys along the valley through Hawridge to Cholesbury, which

The small hamlet of Asheridge never had a service by London Transport, but in February 1971, London Country introduced two morning journeys to Chesham which were added to the 348 timetable by extending short journeys to and from Bellingdon. The service initially ran six days a week, but the Saturday journeys were withdrawn in October 1972, although the Monday to Friday service lasted until the major changes of November 1975. On 6th June that year, BL 17 has reversed at Asheridge for the return to Chesham (Mike Harris)

RF 146 climbs up Gore Hill away from Amersham garage on the 3.56pm 332 journey from Quill Hall to Beaconsfield and Penn. This journey ran only on schooldays and served the schools on Stanley Hill, clearly shown on the blind. The 332 and 398 to Penn were both withdrawn in the major changes of November 1975. RF 146 was Amersham's last RF but was transferred to Garston in July 1976 for a period on the 309 before final withdrawal in March 1977. It went to a dealer and after several owners, I was part of the group who restored it 35 years later in the bus livery it carries in this picture, in which guise it has attended many of our running days when occasionally I have been fortunate enough to drive it. (Colin Fradd)

were used to run a loop from there round Buckland Common and St Leonards, in turn allowing the long established section from Bellingdon to St Leonards to be abandoned completely. The former St Leonards route was shortened to terminate at Bellingdon with the Monday to Friday service cut from 12 to eight journeys, from seven to six Saturdays, and the short lived extension of a couple of Monday to Friday journeys from Bellingdon to Asheridge withdrawn as well. Lee Common, Ballinger and Hyde Heath had been served for a few years by circular route 348 running every two hours in opposite directions from Chesham giving a good service, but the route was now reduced to just four journeys as far as Hyde End only, the Monday to Friday service being left with only one morning return trip into Chesham for shopping. The 359 which had run from Amersham to Great Missenden and Lee Common was extended on into Chesham but, again with fewer journeys than the previous 348 timetable. What was particularly notable were the departure times of the last buses on the rural routes from Chesham on Saturday afternoons at 4.40pm to Tring, 4.31pm to Hyde End, 4.05pm to Lee Common and Great Missenden, and 5.28pm to Bellingdon, there being no demand at all after the last shoppers had returned home. Beyond Coleshill on the 398 to Beaconsfield and Penn, passengers were almost non-existent. The former timetable of ten Monday to Friday and eight Saturday journeys had been a significant over-provision and was withdrawn completely, the route being cut short at Coleshill. The only service left into Beaconsfield was a morning and afternoon peak and schools service plus one return shopping journey on Tuesdays and Thursdays. The road between Beaconsfield and Penn which had had as many as eleven journeys during the week was reduced to just Tuesday and Thursday morning shopping journeys run by the Amersham bus off the 398. The new timetables were compiled so that they could be interworked by the absolute minimum number of buses, but this did not provide the most convenient timings for shopping trips. The gap between journeys into Tring on Saturdays for example meant a stay of just over three hours either morning or afternoon which was far longer than needed for a visit to the shops. The once busy 336 to Rickmansworth and Watford had already been cut back to Rickmansworth on Saturdays, but with these changes it was cut back to just a short shuttle service to Latimer with six journeys going a little further to turn in Chenies. Although these were hourly, the first bus from Chenies into Amersham was as late as 11.38am, and the last one back was at 4.06pm, a timetable almost guaranteed to dissuade any remaining shoppers. By August 1975 cuts had reduced Amersham's run out on its rural routes to only nine buses which included several cross workings on routes such as 305, 336 and 353. The total was even smaller on Saturday when only six buses were required, whilst Sunday required only one SM for the 362 to High Wycombe and two SMs for the 353 to Windsor. Following the reductions mentioned above, there were further minor adjustments which took out two more buses from the Monday to Friday allocation for the rural routes when the April 1976 allocations were put into effect, together with two fewer on Saturdays from the more important services.

Every summer, race days at Epsom involved Country Buses carrying large numbers of people from Epsom station up to the racecourse on the Downs. Almost every garage across the southern area (and sometimes from further afield) supplied buses to run the service. Buses would run directly to Epsom station while others would run from their home garage to the racecourse and back to Epsom. Inspectors would then load each bus in turn as it filled up and send them on their way. RT 3502 has come from Crawley as it heels over into the stone track where passengers alighted. (Peter Horner)

After the 408, 418, 468, and 470 had been converted to omo, Leatherhead retained RTs on the 406 and a few peak hour crew workings on other routes. The 481 schedules included odd peak hour crew workings, and on 6th June 1973, RT 3153 runs into Epsom from Wells Estate on one of these. It carries a 408 number in the canopy blind so probably worked from Leatherhead to Epsom before its journeys on the 481. RT 3153 was one of a batch of 19 new RTs which went to Leatherhead in May 1950, but saw service at several garages before returning in 1972 for its last period in service (Mike Harris)

The 414 was reduced to hourly Monday to Saturday beyond Reigate to Horsham, apart from a limited number of extra journeys as far as Dorking and Capel. During the week, there was no evening service to Croydon after around 6.00pm, and on Sundays the timetable had been reduced to an hourly headway over the whole route. The 405 Sunday service north of Redhill had gone, so that the hourly 414 was all that remained from there to Croydon.

The 1955 frequencies on the Croydon to Chelsham section were in fact better than shown during peak hours as there were several duplicates, additional journeys timed within two or three minutes of each other, and additional buses on the 403 Express service. On Sunday afternoon some 17 additional journeys were operated to and from Warlingham Park Hospital during afternoon visiting times whilst the ten minute headway ran all day until the last bus from Croydon at 11.05pm. In 1955, the 409 also ran some additional peak hour duplicates.

Perhaps the biggest reduction was from Croydon to Godstone where the general headway was halved, whilst on Sunday only an hourly headway remained. Beyond Leatherhead the 408 and 470 were only hourly, although there were additional daytime journeys as far as Effingham on the 408.

Whilst the obvious reductions speak for themselves, the network of major routes radiating from Croydon had once accounted for no less than one seventh of London Transport's entire allocation of Country area RTs – more than 90 being required at maximum. Over 20 years, the cumulative reduction in the number of buses rostered to these routes had been dramatic. The table below shows the declining allocations every five years over this 20-year period

THE CROYDON TRUNK ROUTES – ALLOCATIONS TO ROUTES

Route	Garage	Monday to Friday					Saturday					Sunday				
		18th May	25th May	30th June	18th July	31st Aug	18th May	25th May	30th June	18th July	31st Aug	18th May	25th May	30th June	18th July	31st Aug
		1955	1960	1965	1970	1975	1955	1960	1965	1970	1975	1955	1960	1965	1970	1975
403/483	Chelsham	15	14	14	13	17	12	8	8	9	13	12	9	5	0	3
	Dunton Green	5	4	6	7	3	5	4	3	3	2	4	2	1	0	0
405	Reigate	8	7	7	12	7	7	7	7	6	4	6	4	4	2	2
	Crawley	3	7	7	6	8	2	7	5	4	4	2	4	4	1	0
408/470	Leatherhead	17	17	17	16	15	15	15	11	11	10	14	12	12	6	6
	Guildford	2	2	2	2	2	2	2	2	2	1	2	2	2	1	1
	Chelsham	8	8	7	6	0	9	9	5	3	0	9	4	4	3	0
409/411	Godstone	20	19	18	15	13	17	15	9	9	7	12	9	6	5	4
	East Grinstead	2	3	2	1	1	2	1	1	1	1	2	2	1	0	0
	Reigate	2	2	2	1	0	2	2	1	1	0	0	0	0	0	0
414	Reigate	8	7	7	8	7	10	6	4	5	5	12	5	5	2	4
	Dorking	3	3	3	3	3	4	3	3	3	2	5	4	3	3	2
TOTALS		93	93	92	90	76	87	79	59	57	49	80	57	47	23	22
GARAGE TOTALS																
	Chelsham	23	22	21	19	17	21	17	13	12	13	18	13	9	3	3
	Dunton Green	5	4	6	7	3	5	4	3	3	2	4	2	1	0	0
	Reigate	18	16	16	21	14	19	15	12	12	9	21	9	10	4	6
	Crawley	3	7	7	6	8	2	7	5	4	4	2	4	4	1	0
	Leatherhead	17	17	17	16	15	15	15	11	11	10	14	12	12	6	6
	Godstone	20	19	18	15	13	17	15	9	9	7	12	9	6	5	4
	Guildford	2	2	2	2	2	2	2	2	2	1	2	2	2	1	1
	East Grinstead	2	3	2	1	1	2	1	1	1	1	2	2	0	0	0
	Dorking	3	3	3	3	3	4	3	3	3	2	5	4	3	3	2
TOTALS		93	93	92	90	76	87	79	59	57	49	80	57	47	23	22

NOTES

18th May 1955 — Monday – Friday; EG also had 1 RF for route 409 peak and school journeys and DS had 1 RF for 414 between Reigate and Dorking

25th May 1960 — Saturday; EG also had 1 crew RF Saturday 'to instructions' for route 409 duplicates to and from Felbridge

The increase in the Crawley 405 allocation comes from the route being extended to Horsham over the 434 route in 1957

18th July 1970 — The buses allocated on Sundays to routes 405 and 414 from Reigate, Dorking and Crawley were omo RFs. Sunday operation of 405 / 414 was converted to omo RF from October 1969

Routes 409 and 411 were converted from RT to RML in October 1965

31st Aug 1975 — 54 crew buses still rostered Monday to Friday (CM 15 RT; DS 3 RCL; EG 1 RML; GD 13 RML; RG 14 RCL; CY 8 RCL)

34 crew buses rostered Saturday (CM 11 RT; DS 2 RCL; EG 1 RML; GD 7 RML; RG 9 RCL; CY 4 RCL) The RG Sunday allocation to 405 includes buses for 430. On Sundays all buses were omo.

The crew buses were not necessarily available and any type might be used. Three of the GD allocation were ex-Southdown LS Queen Marys Mon-Fri and 1 Sat.

The drop from 80 crew RT to 22 omo buses on Sundays over 20 years is the most notable; notable also is the dramatic reduction on Saturdays. The overall Monday to Friday total had not been reduced as greatly, but the evening service required fewer than 60 buses, the remainder being rostered only for peak journeys and some day time augmentation.

The losses on the 716 and 716A mentioned above were being repeated over the whole of the Green Line network which was already in serious decline when London Country inherited it in 1970. By 1975 the decline had in reality reached the point where it would be terminal if the network was allowed to continue as it was. The conversion of all routes to omo begun by London Transport was complete (except for the 709) by April 1972, but although this brought desperately needed cost savings, it did nothing to halt the decline. The first Leyland Nationals, although reliable, had been a disaster for the Green Line image, and the Reliances and Swifts were the opposite – they presented an improved image but proved unreliable in service. Traffic congestion continued to affect time-keeping badly, and with many routes having been reduced either partly or completely to hourly headways, passengers were rightly becoming more frustrated at delays. London Country surveyed the system in April 1973 and found that almost no coaches arrived on time at their main central London points, around three quarters being up to ten minutes late, with the remainder anything up to half an hour or more behind schedule. On a journey into London, a delay of five or ten minutes might not be inconvenient, but an extended wait for the return journey was. To add to these woes, vehicle and staff shortages from 1974 onwards resulted in random cancellation of journeys without notice, and it was impossible to warn intending passengers along the route that a particular journey had been cancelled. On a route with an hourly headway, where one journey was cancelled without notice and the next might be running late, passengers were understandably driven away in increasing numbers by such unreliability. Losses were increasing, and by 1973 no fewer than eight Green Line routes were inherently unprofitable, apart from a short period during main school summer holidays when loadings increased. To reinforce the point, even Dorking's routes with their link to Boxhill had fallen into the loss making category.

Despite the delivery of new RPs and SMs in 1971 and 1972, Addlestone managed to retain a few RFs to cover for the inevitable non-availability of the new vehicles, and RFs on Green Line duties became commonplace. RF 72 spent time at Addlestone in 1973 and is working a 716A to Woking, passing a convertible MGB which was a very popular sports car at the time. The bus later went to Dorking where it was delicensed at the beginning of 1975, to be cannibalised for spares before going to Booths at Rotherham for scrap.
(Capital Transport)

The 708 was one of the loss making routes referred to in the text, and was converted from RF to the dreadful first batch of SNCs with thin plastic bus seats. In 1975 they were moved on and replaced by the more comfortable semi-coach SNCs with better seats and luggage racks, and when quite new, SNC 201 waits to pull out onto the main A22 at Blindley Heath working a northbound 708. The Green Line service to East Grinstead would eventually be abandoned in October 1979. (Ian Pringle)

Shortages of staff, unreliable vehicles and delays were significantly damaging Green Line services even by 1973. Staff shortage at Staines garage was one example where it was found impossible to continue to run the remaining 702 journeys to Sunningdale on a regular basis. These were little used anyway and were abandoned in July that year so that resources could be more reliably employed on the main 701 timetable. Where it was possible, minor efforts were made to improve some routes and the 727 and 720 were both extended to Luton and Stansted airports respectively. The Rickmansworth to High Wycombe section of the 724 was proving marginal, so in June 1972 it was diverted to Staines to provide a 30-minute joint headway with the 727 between St Albans and Heathrow, a section of route which remained busy, even requiring duplication at times. But apart from these few changes, and the withdrawal of some outer end sections of route, the network was largely unchanged since its reinstatement at the end of the Second World War, the overriding factor being that the network had not

Advertising provided much needed additional revenue, and several buses appeared at various time in all-over advertising. This particularly garish repaint on RMC 1516 was for the large department store in the centre of Welwyn Garden City which Hatfield's buses passed frequently. It looks particularly unattractive. (Capital Transport)

Continuing reductions in the numbers of conductors threw up many odd crew workings as many older staff saw out their remaining time until retirement. Many of these were peak journeys on otherwise omo routes, and these pictures illustrate two of these.

TOP By 1975 the 423A works journeys to the Wells factory near Dartford were down to one at lunchtime with another on Friday afternoon only, the service being finally withdrawn completely at the end of August that year. On 22nd July, five weeks before the end, RMC 1479 has reversed into the turning point on the lunchtime journey. The original compulsory stop flag is still fixed to the telegraph pole. (Mike Harris)

BOTTOM One of the most wasteful duties was the first journey each morning to Bishops Stortford on the 351, the bus returning to Hertford as a 350. This remarkable working lasted until late May 1976, and a couple of weeks before that on 7th May, RMC 1474 has just left Bishops Stortford on the 7.39am 350 to Hertford. From Sele Farm Estate it will work the 8.51am back to Fairfax Road garage where it will remain idle all day until a late afternoon journey to Buntingford on the 331. These were the last truly 'rural' double deck crew duties in the Country Area. (Mike Harris)

responded to the public's changing travel patterns. One of Green Line's traditional attractions had been its links through London's outer suburbs to both central London and Home Counties beauty spots and towns, and with 15 or 30-minute headways seven days a week it was both cheap and attractive. Even by the mid-1960s however, car ownership had greatly reduced the demand, and traffic delays had badly eroded reliability, to the extent that by the mid-1970s the only demand remaining was for a reducing number of regular commuters, and a scant number of leisure journeys which were generally becoming shorter. Suburban rail links into London, which were much quicker but had traditionally been more expensive, became progressively more attractive as Green Line fares steadily increased and frequencies were cut back. Although the retrenchment in Green Line timetables had been a commercial necessity, it did not change the underlying fact that on top of all the other issues, the actual route network itself had become largely irrelevant.

The 309 timetable saw successive reductions after 1970. There were eight different turning points in Harefield, that at Hill End having the least service. The Saturday journeys were withdrawn completely in 1973 leaving just two shopping journeys into Rickmansworth during the week although the timing of these were hopelessly inconvenient for the last remaining shoppers. RF 614 has just reversed into Waybeards Farm entrance at the terminus and will wait outside the Vernon Arms pub out of shot on the right. It has the full blind showing two intermediate points for the short 18 minute journey. The section of the 309 between Rickmansworth and Harefield was replaced on September 1977 by a route numbered 128 won by LT in a tender from Hillingdon Council. RF 614 was withdrawn from Garston in March 1976 and sold six months later to Booths. (Mike Harris)

The crisis brought about by increasing numbers of unserviceable vehicles came to a head during 1975 and resulted in further Green Line cuts. After the 702 had been withdrawn, the 701 continued to lose money, and was abandoned at short notice in October 1975 so that precious resources could be devoted to keeping other routes running. The situation at Staines garage was so bad that the SNCs from the 701 had to be kept back simply to provide cover for the desperate condition of its RPs which it ran on the 718 and 724. Staines had only eight RPs allocated, and required all eight on a daily basis which, with their poor reliability and lack of spare parts, was an impossible task. Indeed, for a period prior to the withdrawal of the 701, only six out of its eight RPs had been serviceable. At least some of Northfleet's SNCs from the other half of the 701 allocation could be used elsewhere, and some went to Chelsham to replace what were the last RFs officially rostered for Green Line service. It had been more than 23 years since that garage had received its first Green Line RFs in April 1952, and in the intervening years, Chelsham's RFs alone had run in excess of 130,000 return journeys on the 706 and 707 to Aylesbury and back with barely a handful of journeys missed. The allocation of the spare SNCs to Chelsham should have been the end of official Green Line RF operation, but they would continue to perform regularly on many routes for some time as cover for their unreliable replacements. Earlier, in May 1975, the 712 and 713 were divided in London. The few remaining peak hour journeys beyond St Albans to Dunstable were withdrawn, and London Country hoped to retain the handful of commuters from north of St Albans by offering through fares on the 342/343 bus route, but this was a forlorn hope. The southern section to Dorking was re-numbered 703, and the revised service perhaps illustrates the point made about the increasing irrelevance of much of the Green Line

Chapter four describes the increasing use of minibuses in the approach to deregulation, but several years earlier in August 1974 London Country introduced an experimental 'dial a ride' service between Harlow bus station and Old Harlow. It was sponsored by Harlow District Council and the Development Corporation together with the Transport Road Research Laboratory in order to test the practicality of such a service. It ran for two years, and at the time was the largest such experiment in the UK. The vehicles used were these Mellor bodied Ford Transits and, during its first week, FT 1 is seen in Harlow New Town Centre. Such buses were later referred to as 'bread vans' given that many of the original bodies were simply adapted from delivery vans until later developments produced bodies which were better designed for passengers. (Capital Transport)

network. The link all the way into London was no longer necessary, and a limited stop route from Dorking to Morden (southern terminus of the Northern Line) would have been cheaper to operate, less prone to traffic delay, and probably no less attractive to passengers. The revised timetable for the 703 had blocks of hourly departures with irregular gaps during the day so that it could be operated by only four coaches. This made it difficult if not impossible for the few regular passengers who remained to memorise times. The last departure from Dorking to London was as early as 6.30pm, and the Sunday service was cut to two-hourly – a quarter of the service level 12 years earlier – and became virtually pointless. The route was already losing money before these changes, and the reductions which came from the revised timetable rendered the route even less attractive to the point where its few remaining passengers abandoned it, so that it was withdrawn completely after only 16 months in October 1977.

RT 3752 nearest the camera and RT 2504 in front were both sent to Stevenage in June 1972 to work the 800 series of town services after they were made redundant at Leatherhead when ANs converted the 408 and 470. RT 3752 has been repainted in the lighter shade of green which London Country experimented with on a few buses and both have the yellow LCBS 'flying polo' logo on the rear side panel. The routes had an extension to Hitchin on Tuesdays and Saturdays together with some afternoon and peak hour journeys during the week, and RT 3752 is working on one of these. Both buses were replaced again by new ANs on 14th October 1972 when the entire Stevenage town network was converted to omo. RT 3752 went to Chelsham for 18 months, then to Garston where it put in its final four years before withdrawal in April 1977. RT 2504 went to Harlow to cover for defective RMLs and ran there for 3 more years until final withdrawal at the end of 1975.

In its first six years, London Country's management had been faced with almost insurmountable difficulties – a poisoned chalice indeed. As described in the next chapter, the average age of the fleet had at least been reduced substantially, but the irony was that of nearly 700 new buses purchased from 1970 onwards, well over a third had proved unreliable and not up to the job required of them. The availability of the Routemaster fleet had been decimated from a lack of spares, and the almost daily unpredictable cancellation of services across most garages was accelerating the continuing decline in passengers. High inflation continued to increase every-day running costs, and interest charges on the large amounts borrowed to invest in new buses were a further unmanageable burden. By the end of 1975, London Country had in reality reached a point of no return unless drastic and radical action was taken. As we shall see however, 1976 was the beginning of what proved to be the eventual successful turnaround of the business.

2 The Turnaround Begins: 1976-1980

In April 1976, the fleet total stood at 1188, of which 494 were former London Transport buses and coaches. There were 108 Merlin MB and MBS buses which were only seven years old but not entirely reliable, 23 of which were unserviceable. The Routemaster fleet totalled 209 buses which were either 11 or 14 years old, 30 of which were off the road. The RT and RF fleet still consisted of 139 buses, all a minimum of 22 years old, and of which 38 were unlicensed or withdrawn, while 16 RTs were licensed only as trainers. Of the overall fleet total, no fewer than 226 (almost one fifth) remained unlicensed, either withdrawn or awaiting repair. Staff turnover and shortages plus the continuing influx of new buses also meant that 47 buses were in use solely as trainers, but a number of RTs had been released from training by the purchase of 20 Burlingham bodied Leyland PD3s from Ribble. This purchase – though useful – proved to be less than satisfactory since around half of them would spend much of 1978 off the road awaiting spares. Although the average age of the fleet had reduced significantly to about 7½ years, the average age of the former LT buses was almost double that. The fact that too great a number of the new buses purchased in its first three or four years were simply not reliable enough for day to day service has already been referred to.

By the start of 1977, the aged RT fleet had been reduced significantly. RT 3607 had been withdrawn at the end of 1976, although it languished out of use at Leatherhead for another 18 months. It was one of a number that had been relicensed as cover for defective RMLs, and sent to Staines in November 1975. Some months before withdrawal, and looking in fine condition after 24 years' service, it stops to pick up passengers on a 441 to Hedgerley Village with a good load. The front via blind box has been masked so that RML blinds can be used, since there were few RT blinds left by then, and a rear number blind has been fitted over the platform. (Ian Pringle)

RT 986 survived into 1977 and in June the previous year it is almost empty as it stops in Bletchingley on a 411 to Croydon, substituting for an RML. This type of blind display was all too common at the time and the chalked number 435 suggests that it had been borrowed by East Grinstead.
(Peter Plummer)

Reigate's last crew work was converted to omo towards the end of 1977, and had included peak hour journeys on the 405B which served the industrial area between Crawley and Gatwick. RCLs replaced RTs on the 405/405B in 1972, and on 26th June 1975 RCL 2259 waits to work an afternoon journey through Crawley and Furnace Green back to Reigate.
(Mike Harris)

RF 175 was Dorking's spare bus until July 1977 when it went to Addlestone to cover for its shortage of SMs. Here it would become one of the last five in service before final withdrawal at the beginning of 1978, having completed 26 years. The 412 route would be lost in major changes in 1985. In late 1976, it has stopped at the White Horse in Dorking showing the unique blind display for the route. Although it terminated at Sutton, this was only ever shown as a qualifying point to Holmbury St Mary so that potential passengers could not confuse the destination with the other Sutton.
(Colin Fradd)

The Welwyn Garden City and Hatfield town services were renumbered into 8xx series in February 1974, and were operated by the dual door long Leyland Nationals. In October 1977, LN 13 is loading at the 'Cherry Tree' stop next to Welwyn Garden City station on a journey via the hospital to Knightsfield on the edge of the town. The routes we re-cast again in May 1978 with G prefix numbers, and during 1979 the LNs were replaced with newer SNBs. Note the original London Transport Q plate under the bus stop with an arrow pointing towards the bus station. (Mike Harris)

The significant cuts to timetables had also reduced the allocations at many garages to the point where their fixed overhead costs were simply unsustainable, and the figures for some of the smaller garages are listed below. The two figures shown represent the separate totals for buses and coaches.

GARAGE	31.10.65	1.1.70	3.4.76
DORKING	19 / 15	16 / 10	11 / 8
LUTON	23 / 8	21 / 4	11 / 4
TRING	8 / 7	10 / 8	8 / 6
EAST GRINSTEAD	16 / 7	16 / 4	13 / 4
GUILDFORD	18 / 9	16 / 7	17 / 7
HIGH WYCOMBE	18 / 8	18 / 10	13 / 5
STAINES	18 / 14	16 / 11	14 / 8
TOTALS	120 / 58	111 / 52	87 / 42

In ten years, the combined bus and coach allocation at these garages had been reduced by 49, and 70% of these reductions had come during the first six years of London Country's management. These garages had never had large allocations in any event, but these reductions meant that they were uneconomic to keep open, and four of them would be closed during the next five years. Luton's allocation in particular had seen savage cuts. Of the biggest garages, even Garston, the largest of all with a capacity of around 100, had seen its allocation fall from 79 to 66 since January 1970.

During 1976, annual losses on the Green Line network alone increased to more than £450,000, and the situation could not be allowed to continue. At April 1976, the Monday to Friday run out still required 177 coaches plus another six for late running spares, which compares with 211 at 1st January 1970. Although it is perhaps a worthless comparison, the difference on Sundays between the 148 scheduled at April 1976 and the 306 twenty years earlier gives a stark illustration of just how much Green Line leisure travel at weekends had declined. Frequencies could not be reduced any further, and the route network had become largely irrelevant in the face of changing travel patterns.

In the autumn of 1976, Derek Fytche was appointed as London Country's new Managing Director and faced the stark reality of the company's dire financial and operational situation. The position had reached the point where only two options were available – either to take radical action or to close down the business completely. It is hardly worth speculating what the result of the latter option would have been, with, presumably, a mass of smaller unco-ordinated operators taking over routes or parts of routes on a piecemeal basis and with a huge increase in public subsidy, even assuming the county councils had the resources and finances available to manage such a situation.

As far as Green Line was concerned, the two options were either to abandon virtually the entire network, or to radically change the image while at the same time making fundamental changes to the routes themselves, and it is to London Country's great credit that the second option was chosen. As far as the Green Line 'brand' was concerned, the influx of new vehicles since 1972 had been a

Within a couple of years after the introduction of the SMAs it is doubtful if there was ever a week when Dartford did not put out an RF on the route, and although they were completely reliable, they were a further factor in the decline of the Green Line image. RF 690, looks drab in all-over NBC green, but with a proper blind as it is about to set off from Windsor Bus Station on a 725 to Dartford. It was one a small number repainted into NBC livery, and was the penultimate 'bus' RF in service, not being withdrawn until September 1977 to become one of 11 RFs sold to Hall's Coaches at Hounslow for use on their airside service at Heathrow. (Peter Plummer)

complete failure. If Green Line was to be a successful limited stop network of coach routes, then proper full coach specification vehicles were necessary, and they had to operate routes that passengers wanted to travel on. So it was that on 28th January 1977, the first change was made when the 712, 713, and 714 between London, St Albans and Luton were withdrawn and replaced by 707 and 717, two new routes between Luton and Victoria which combined the parts of the previous ones which might carry the most passengers and be subject to the least of the inevitable traffic delays. Luton Airport was served from the start, and an hourly headway ran seven days a week. Evening services had been little used during the week, so that the last departure from London was 7.43pm, and there was no early morning Sunday service, so that the new timetable far better reflected likely passenger usage. The former sections through Park Street and Radlett, and from Finchley into Kings Cross and Baker Street were abandoned, interchange with the Underground at Golders Green was maintained, whilst perhaps most significant of all was that the new routes served Brent Cross Shopping Centre. Out of town regional shopping centres were then in their infancy, but it was precisely the sort of new destination that Green Line routes needed to serve to encourage passengers to return. Many former intermediate stops were discontinued so that there were only 25 stops in total between London and Luton Airport. Combined with the more direct routeing, around 15 minutes was saved on the end to end running time and, with sensible layovers at each end, only four coaches were needed to run the whole timetable. London Country had decided to lease the new coaches on a five-year basis so that over time, no coach would be older than five years, and the new AEC Reliance 'heavyweight' coaches were everything that the Green Line image badly needed. Internally, they were to full coach specification, and despite the strict NBC corporate livery rules, London Country wisely decided to depart from this so that the coaches appeared in a smart new livery which was modern but at the same time reflected the traditional Green Line image.

Dartford's allocation of SMAs for its share of the 725 Green Line were frequently used on bus routes, and SMA 18 climbing up from Watchgate back to Dartford on the 423. Although it still retains its original livery, the LCBS logo on the front panel has been replaced with the white National fleetname which does not enhance its appearance. (Colin Fradd)

Among many revisions at the beginning of 1977, Hemel Hempstead's town services were completely revised, all routes being given an H prefix. Eighteen MBSs were rostered with five SNBs cross-working from other routes. The closure of Tring garage a few months later threw up spare Nationals which, together with others, were fitted with fareboxes and gradually replaced the MBSs so that only six remained by November 1977. MBS 407 survived to be one of the last pair in service at Hemel Hempstead, not being delicensed until December 1978. It is picking up passengers at Grove Hill with one of the replacement SNCs on route H4 in the background. (John Miller)

Green Line route 700 was started in 1977 as an express service to Windsor, picking up at a few London stops before running non-stop along the M4 to Windsor. Initially it ran as a summer only service but from 1978 ran all year together with another new route 701 serving Heathrow and running on to Windsor Safari Park in the summer. RB 20 was one of the new fleet of coaches which were a major factor in Green Line's recovery, and is at Windsor bus station between trips in 1977. The more luxurious nature of these coaches is obvious, their only small drawback being the limited size of the destination display which was difficult to read from any distance. (Ian Pringle)

The introduction of the new 707 and 717 routes also precipitated the closure of Luton garage. Luton's allocation had halved from 31 to 15 during the previous decade, and the loss of its share of the 714 route was the final blow to a garage which had always been on the outer edge of the network and never had a large allocation. Its bus operations had fallen away, and although its allocation to the main 321 trunk route had remained stable, timetables on its other bus routes had reduced to the point where only four buses were required to run them, compared with 15 when London Country had taken over. The cuts in February 1971 referred to earlier, when Bedfordshire declined to support the 364A, were followed in July 1972 by the abandonment of the 365 to Wheathampstead and St Albans, and a year later the 364 to Hitchin. The withdrawal of the 714 had already been preceded by the loss of some staff who had transferred to United Counties' Luton depot as the scheduled work reduced, and Luton's closure became inevitable. Before the loss of the 714, the former 364 route to Hitchin had a couple of uncertain years after London Country withdrew, being first replaced by Court Line who were the major package deal holiday company based at Luton Airport. They soon went into administration, to be replaced by Jey-Son who equally failed, and who had also run some journeys on the old Birch Brothers 205 route through Peters Green to Kimpton which had not survived Birch's takeover by United Counties in 1969. Jey-Son gave up the Hitchin route in December 1974 after which United Counties took over using the 88 route number, running five or six journeys a day, but in a bizarre development it was London Country which replaced the other route as far as Kimpton. It was numbered 365 and ran three journeys Friday and Saturday only, the lunchtime and afternoon journeys on Saturday being extended to Codicote. It was the last London Country route officially rostered for RF operation, and because of the reduction of other crew work at Luton the three Saturday journeys were officially crew operated. The lunchtime journeys were also notable for the fact that the bus had a 67-minute layover at Kimpton on Friday and 51 minutes at Codicote on Saturdays. Quite how anybody thought that this service was worth continuing is difficult to imagine, but United Counties took over operation of the route after Luton closed. As noted in the next chapter the route was later extended from Codicote to Stevenage, restoring a service through Nup End which had ceased when the 329 had been abandoned more than six years earlier.

London Country put much effort into marketing the new 707/717, and they were an immediate success. Encouraged by this, during the next couple of years several of the long standing routes were replaced by innovative new ones, while others were cut back or withdrawn. In April 1977, three months after the 707/717 started, Chelsham lost its Green Line allocation when the long standing 706 was withdrawn. Passenger usage from London to the south of Croydon was minimal, and the local Croydon to Chelsham section was easily covered by the frequent 403 bus route, although the 706 routeing had been slightly different. The northern outer end from Hemel Hempstead to Aylesbury was covered by extending the 708, and in doing so created the longest Green Line route in terms of end-to-end running time which became 4hrs 6mins during the day. The withdrawal of the 706 also removed Tring's Green Line workings, leaving it with only eight buses Monday to Friday, seven Saturday, and nothing at all Sunday, so that closure was inevitable. All Tring's buses were rostered to the 301, 302 and 312, with workings on the local 387, and it was easy to transfer these to Hemel Hempstead which had always run the bulk of these routes. Three former Tring Green Line workings were also transferred to Hemel Hempstead to run additional peak hour journeys to and from London over and above the 708 hourly headway. The long running time on the 708 though gave rise to problems scheduling drivers. East Grinstead's drivers worked only as far as Hemel Hempstead where a local driver would then take the coach to Aylesbury and back. To minimise the total number of coaches required, the timetable only allowed ten minutes layover at Aylesbury, so late running from London meant the Hemel driver having to try to catch up time with little chance of recovery at Aylesbury. By the time the East Grinstead driver took over again at Hemel Hempstead for the return journey, it might well already be late even before the long run through the northern suburbs and central London. At East Grinstead, the schedule allowed Hemel Hempstead drivers around 50 minutes break on most journeys, but late running could easily eat into this, causing a delay in the departure of the return journey. Traffic delays on a route this long simply worsened the operational difficulties, and after only 11 months at the beginning of April 1978, the southern section of the 719 from London to Wrotham

The 708 had a brief period of operation with RMCs but was converted back to RF in October 1968 so that it could be converted to omo on a joint timetable with the 706. RF 94 is nearing the end of the long run from East Grinstead as it turns off the A41 opposite Two Water garage towards Hemel Hempstead town centre. It was based at East Grinstead when London Country took over and remained on the 708 until SNCs arrived in 1973 at which point it went to Chelsham for further service on the 706, finally being withdrawn at the end of 1974. (Capital Transport)

was abandoned and diverted instead to East Grinstead, allowing the 708 to be cut to a London to Aylesbury service which operationally, was far more manageable. Wrotham had always been an impractical boundary with Maidstone & District resultant from the 1933 Act. The Green Line route should logically have gone another mile into Borough Green which offered greater traffic potential and where there were frequent rail links to London, but Maidstone & District's 122 route covered this, and so London Transport had always terminated at Wrotham. This created a 'dead leg' south of Farningham which was the last real traffic objective, and whilst the bouyant period until the mid-1950s had once made the route viable, the long decline after that rendered the Wrotham section increasingly pointless. With the end of the 719, a few extra journeys were added on the 423 bus route out to West Kingsdown to maintain some link with the railway at Swanley, but the end of the Green Line route severed the regular link to Wrotham from Swanley. After withdrawal of the 719, Maidstone & District altered their Tenterden to London coach route to run as a part replacement, which they numbered 919 running five journeys a day through Wrotham. London Country however, somehow felt the need to continue with a Monday to Friday peak service numbered 729 consisting of just one morning and one afternoon journey and which – with great irony – was extended beyond Wrotham to Borough Green! While the times of London Country's 729 filled gaps between the M&D service, the evening return journey from Borough Green back to Swanley garage was timed to run three minutes behind a 919 journey, thus guaranteeing it would run empty the whole way. It is not recorded how many commuters used the 729 during its short period of operation!

Another change In January 1977 was the withdrawal of the 310A to Rye House in Hoddesdon together with the 327 which ran via St Margarets and Rye House to Hoddesdon and Nazeing. They were partly replaced by a diversion from the main 310 route, numbered 316. The 310/310A had been converted to omo with ANs in 1972 but perennial shortages saw daily unofficial crew operation until 1978. Although a few sets of intermediate RT blinds for the 316 were produced, RT 4792 hasn't been fitted with them and shows shabby blinds with half of a 'Private' display and a chalked route number. The bus spent its last year at Hertford before withdrawal in March 1977, and a few weeks before that waits at Ware Crossing on a 316 to Enfield. The conductor no longer has a Gibson ticket machine but has been issued with a Setright used for many years by Green Line conductors. (Ian Pringle)

It was also no surprise in the Green Line review that the 721 Brentwood to London service was finally abandoned. In the halcyon days more than two decades earlier, Romford garage had put out 32 double deckers on the 721 and 722 on a five or ten minute headway all day into Aldgate. Traffic, car ownership, and electrification of the parallel railway had unrelentingly eaten away passengers, and after the 722 had finally been abandoned in 1968, the 721 declined further still. By 1977, when London Country began the re-launch of the Green Line network, Romford's run out for the 721 was just six coaches plus four for the 724. In 1976, the daytime 15 minute headway on the 721 had been halved in a last effort to reduce costs, and London Country had attempted to agree more competitive fares between Romford and London with London Transport. Both these initiatives failed however and, on 1st July 1977, the 721 was withdrawn, Romford garage closed, and its share of the 724 transferred to Harlow. Earlier, in April, in another innovative change, the 720 into Aldgate which had attracted no subsidy was also withdrawn. The section through the east London suburbs into Aldgate with its terrible traffic was pointless, and the 702 and 703 which replaced the 720 from Bishop's Stortford ran alternately to Walthamstow Central to connect with the Underground, or to Waltham Cross which was a viable shopping destination. This illustrated perfectly what might have been done many years earlier by London Transport with some imaginative changes, providing new routes which gave connections passengers could benefit from, and at the same time avoiding the worst of the traffic congestion.

The southern section of the 704 was a good example of a route which had become increasingly irrelevant. Heavy traffic as far as Bromley was also a serious problem so that late running was commonplace with little opportunity to catch up by the time Sevenoaks was reached. In 1977 RP 67 swings into Sevenoaks bus station working a 704 to Tunbridge Wells. It is 30 minutes late, and the Windsor driver who would normally have changed for his break at Tonbridge will come off here while a spare Dunton Green driver takes the coach to Tunbridge Wells and back. (Alan Charman)

Following cuts to Green Line schedules at the end of 1968, Grays received some RMCs to replace RTs on bus routes. The 723 had been converted to omo in January 1972, and survived the radical Green Line review for a few years. GY80 was a morning peak duty from Grays to East Ham, and an oddity of scheduling resulted in this being crew worked until RMC operation at Grays ended in the summer of 1979. Here, RMC 1476 stops in Belhus Estate on a snowy morning working this duty. (Peter Plummer)

Union agreements with London Transport had historically prevented the cross-London Green Line routes being cut in half in London, but new agreements were gradually reached to permit this, and by March 1978, only four of the original cross London routes were still running. Further changes over the next 18 months culminated in the 715 Guildford to Hertford and 719 Hemel Hempstead to East Grinstead routes being the last cross London routes, and both ceased at the end of October 1979, almost 49 years since the first cross London routes had begun in December 1930. The 715 was split into two routes with the London to Hertford section numbered 735 and reduced to an hourly service with some gaps of 90 minutes. The commuter rail services that mostly paralleled the Hertford route had dealt a heavy blow to passenger numbers, and the much reduced 735 was a fraction of the 20-minute headway 16 years earlier. The southern section though fared better, with a 30-minute headway between Guildford and Kingston, generally hourly beyond there into London, plus the addition of some express commuter journeys. The 719 was cut back to its original Hemel Hempstead to London service, with the southern half to East Grinstead being withdrawn. The road from Croydon to East Grinstead had always been paralleled by the 409 bus route, and now this was revised to include an hourly 'express' service to East Grinstead. On the same day, the few remaining journeys on the 709 were withdrawn as London Country had reached the point where it could not save any more costs on the four Monday to Friday peak journeys and the two on Sunday.

The Monday to Friday journeys had been relatively costly to run since the two drivers needed worked a spreadover duty, which cost more money, and with revenue having fallen well below costs, and neither Surrey or GLC being prepared to offer a subsidy, withdrawal remained the only option. The withdrawal of the 709 and 719 marked a significant milestone which went unnoticed, since they had represented the last Green Line operation between central London and Croydon which had once been an important link, with six coaches an hour, all day, seven days a week right up until the 710 was withdrawn in October 1968. After this, the remaining service on the 706 and 708 (and later 719) continued to maintain two or three coaches per hour for the next 8½ years and was a further example of the network failing to react to changing travel patterns in providing a link through London suburbs which was no longer relevant.

The success of the revitalised Green Line network encouraged London Country to bring forward the introduction of the new coaches. Originally, 150 coaches would have arrived at 30 per year over a five year period, but accelerating this allowed new coaches to replace less satisfactory SNCs and RPs. The SNCs were generally reliable and were redeployed on bus routes, so that most of the RPs still running could be withdrawn or kept as spares, and by August 1979, only 2½ years after the first new routes had been introduced, 120 of the new Reliance coaches were in service. By then half the RP fleet were withdrawn and the ones left on Green Line work were mostly confined to Hertford, Harlow, Guildford and Addlestone with a few others as spares or rostered to bus routes. In time, new destinations like Oxford, Brighton, Cambridge, Reading, Southend and even Northampton were reached, often on joint routes with neighbouring operators, and within five years the Green Line network had been transformed and turned around. Some new ventures such as the suburban 734 from Hertford to Addlestone were unsuccessful, but it was the innovative approach, although perhaps long overdue, which saved the operation.

The 466 was a minor route from Staines to Knowle Hill running mostly to an hourly headway and was one of those requiring increasing support. It was always rostered for omo RF and was restricted to single deck working due to two low bridges on the road into Knowle Hill. RP 44 is seen near Virginia Water and is probably working an early morning journey before its day on the 718, or substituting for an unserviceable RF. (Colin Fradd)

Following their approaches in 1975 to councils in the northern area, London Country wrote to Surrey County Council in 1976 to highlight that fewer than a third of its routes operating in Surrey were sufficiently viable without increasing levels of support. In November 1975, the section of the 416 between Leatherhead and Esher had been abandoned in favour of a limited minibus service operated by Mole Valley Transport, but now more widespread reductions were essential. One of these was the 432 from Guildford to Great Bookham, which was unusual in that, although it served a reasonable population and provided links to the railway at Effingham Junction and Bookham, this was a particularly affluent part of Surrey with many large expensive houses along the route and where incomes and car ownership were exceptionally high. The hourly headway had been halved over the years, the evening and Sunday service abandoned, and the Saturday timetable reduced to just five journeys, so that further savings on the 432 were impossible without total withdrawal and Surrey County Council looked critically at whether a subsidy for the route should continue at all. Tillingbourne had begun to overcome many of their difficulties and were looking at ways to expand their business, as part of which they offered to take over the 432. This came to nothing at the time, and subsequently London Country extended the Boxhill to Leatherhead route to Great Bookham and on over the 432 to Guildford, which gave some additional links into Leatherhead and was cheaper to operate with more efficient use of buses. Reductions in the 412 and the retirement of a couple of the Holmbury St Mary drivers had rendered the outstation there redundant, and its use ceased in November 1975 after 48 years. In their continuing efforts to expand, Tillingbourne made a bold move in May 1976 when they extended the 448 from Peaslake back to Ewhurst and on into Cranleigh, an extension which came about from a passenger survey of routes in the Cranleigh area that identified a potential demand from Gomshall and Peaslake. Cranleigh was expanding and becoming a useful shopping destination, and the revised route could also provide a link to the railway at Gomshall as there had been no station at Cranleigh since the Guildford to Horsham branch line had been shut in 1965 as part of the 'Beeching' cuts. The extended 448 therefore provided attractive new links, and in time was linked to another route back into Guildford via Bramley to give what would become a successful venture. While this had nothing much to do with London Country at the time, it was perhaps the start of Tillingbourne's return to stability which in time gave them a foothold to successfully challenge both London Country and Alder Valley on their networks in the area

I have already referred to the fact that London Country had inherited an infrastructure which had too many garages. Green Line reductions were the catalyst for the closure of Luton and Tring, and High Wycombe followed at the end of September 1977. Many of High Wycombe's workings on bus routes had always been shared with Amersham, and the 711 Green Line was by then beyond saving as it was. Indeed, staff shortages, and others transferring to Alder Valley at High Wycombe had left the 711 running to an ad-hoc emergency timetable during 1977 so its final withdrawal was the only realistic option. By 1977, High Wycombe's allocation had been reduced to only 13 buses, so closing that instead of Amersham was the sensible commercial decision. The November 1975 cuts in Amersham's rural network have already been covered, but since it remained operational, albeit with a few more timetable reductions, it was probably better to move everything into Amersham rather than retain High Wycombe where town service workings, some of which were already jointly run with Alder Valley, could readily

The 440 was a semi rural route requiring increased subsidy, but with Caterham along the line of route it retained an hourly headway throughout the 1970s, although it would eventually be drastically cut back MBS 4 was part of a batch of 15 experimental standee buses delivered in 1966, initially for the central London 'Red Arrow' routes, while the last of the batch XMB 15 was intended for the country area. London Country exchanged XMB 15 for MBS 4 in 1973 and it was one of Reigate's last before going to Crawley in February 1977, and later Leatherhead before being withdrawn in 1979. It stands at the terminus outside the Monotype factory at Salfords on a section of route which was withdrawn and diverted to the new Whitebushes Estate in 1977. (Capital Transport)

SM 108 was new to Leatherhead in June 1970 when the 418/418A were converted. It was repainted into NBC livery in 1976, and comes along Bookham Common having just left Bookham Station on a 418 to Kingston. The upper case lettering for the intermediate points on the later style of blinds looked cramped. A few years after this picture was taken, this section of the 418 was withdrawn along with the 432, to be replaced by extending the 416 through to Guildford. SM 108 was withdrawn in 1977 when only seven years old, and the original LT request stop complete with fare stage plate and timetable frame outlived it by some time! (John Miller)

Short journeys on the 408 terminating at Effingham had turned in a lay-by at Woodlands Road on the main road to Guildford, but in February 1978 they were extended a short distance off the main road into Effingham village to turn at the Sir Douglas Haig Pub, providing a better link to Leatherhead. Although the 432 also served this point, it terminated at Great Bookham requiring a change to the 418 to travel to Leatherhead. In June that year, AN 125 has arrived at the Effingham terminus from Croydon and the driver is filling in his waybill before the return journey. (Ian Pringle)

Sometime in 1976, an almost empty SM 124 comes along the road between Seer Green and Chalfont St Giles on a 305 to Uxbridge, a route which was run jointly between Amersham and High Wycombe. It is a High Wycombe bus, and although Amersham received new SMs for its share of the 305 in 1971, it was not until the early part of 1976 that a few SMs were transferred to High Wycombe to replace its MBs. Amersham took over the whole route after High Wycombe closed. (Mike Harris)

be taken over by them completely. Moving High Wycombe's remaining work to Amersham resulted in no small amount of dead mileage running buses to and from High Wycombe for service, but the costs of this were still substantially less than keeping the fixed overhead of an unnecessary garage.

As part of the regeneration of the Green Line network, the 711 was replaced with a new London – High Wycombe – Oxford route operated jointly with City of Oxford. There was an irony that London Country's share was worked remotely from Amersham, thus bringing Green Line workings back to Amersham five years after the last 710 had run in September 1972. The southern end of the 711 was partly replaced by a new bus route numbered 422 from Reigate but operating only as far as Sutton, since the section through south London into central London had long become, like all the other traditional routes, of no interest to passengers. Although Reigate lost their contribution to the 711, they retained the 727 which remained profitable, still requiring some duplication on the southern section to and from Heathrow.

Among the many changes which followed the closure of High Wycombe garage was a new Green Line route from London to Oxford worked jointly with City of Oxford. It was one of the new routes which broke down the former rigid barriers of the 1933 Act and brought Green Line work back to Amersham garage. RB 99 waits at Gloucester Green bus station in Oxford to work a 290 journey to London while a similar coach belonging to Oxford waits behind. (UK Bus Photos)

London Transport converted the 484 Slough town service to omo in 1969 with MBSs, which London Country continued to use on the route for several years. The use of an SM on the route was unusual, and SM 464 has stopped in Slough High Street in September 1974 on the way to Langley Village. It has been borrowed from Addlestone, probably to cover for a defective MBS which was ironic considering the unreliability of the SMs, and the text refers to three quarters of them being withdrawn by the end of 1979. (Mike Harris)

The long awaited new Central Works at Crawley finally opened in January 1976 and at last allowed a gradual improvement – if slow at first – in London Country's ability to work through the backlog of repairs and re-certifications. Its opening was, in fact, probably the major factor which eventually solved the service reliability issues caused by long term vehicle unavailability. The delivery of new Leyland Nationals also at last began to speed up in 1976. After early teething problems, the National had become a success, and because the NBC specified it as their principal large single decker, it had been in great demand, to the extent that British Leyland's Workington factory which built them could not keep up. None of London Country's 1975 order had been delivered in the year, adding further to the pressure of unserviceable buses, but with production catching up, the 30 which had been delayed from 1975 were added to the 32 of the 1976 order, so that all 62 new Nationals were in service by the end of that year. The poor reliability of new buses – particularly the Swifts and Reliances, and to a lesser extent the Merlins – combined with the lack of spares had also caused London Country to re-think its requirements for new vehicles. The Routemaster fleet was by then 10 or 11 years old with the RMCs 14 years old and coming to the end of their normal life span. They had suffered particularly badly from the spares crisis, and given the objective of 100% omo across the fleet, it was not worthwhile to keep too many of these crew operated buses in service any longer. London Country therefore decided that Leyland Nationals should be purchased in increasing numbers both to maintain the push towards 100% omo and to replace the less reliable new buses, so that 90 were therefore ordered for delivery in 1977. With more Atlanteans coming into stock it was at last possible to improve reliability. The Swifts had performed so poorly that 45 (one third) of them were withdrawn in 1978 when only seven or eight years old and 55 more in 1979. The RPs had proved equally unreliable and were still suffering badly from a lack of spares, so that over time only half of them could be recertified. Even this took almost two years to achieve, whilst the rest were abandoned and never ran again in service. These too were only six years old, not even half way through a normal service life, and represented the worst of British Leyland's poor quality and lack of reliability in so many of their products from the early 1970s.

The picture of BN 48 in chapter one refers to the reductions to the 464, 465 and 485 in August 1975. In the same changes, the 485 was extended from Edenbridge, replacing the 434 to East Grinstead which in turn was left just with odd peak journeys as far as Dormansland. SNC 72 was quickly downgraded to bus work and transferred to East Grinstead early in 1976. It waits to turn onto the A25 at Westerham Green on a 485 to East Grinstead. These former Green Line buses would be augmented by increasing numbers of new series B buses to replace double deckers. (Colin Fradd)

By 1978 there was an irony that many other NBC subsidiaries, having ordered quantities of new Leyland Nationals, found that they were surplus to requirements even before delivery as they continued to make more service cuts. This provided London Country with an opportunity to acquire large numbers, and in the 18 months up to the end of 1979, 168 further Nationals were delivered, all of which were the updated 'B Series'. These had been developed by British Leyland as a cheaper version and were to the shorter 10.3 metre length, intended for rural work, and at £25,000 each were about 10% cheaper than the former standard model. These, together with another 80 Atlanteans which arrived in 1978, at last solved vehicle shortages, but this threw up so many withdrawn unserviceable buses that London Country found itself with insufficient storage space. Some of the larger garage yards such as Grays, Hertford and Chelsham had become 'graveyards' for withdrawn buses, but there were so many that space had to be rented on an old airfield in Hertfordshire to store them all awaiting sale. In early 1977, London Country found itself in the unexpected position of being able to benefit from London Transport's problems, where they were experiencing difficulties of their own with the large numbers of DM/DMS Fleetlines and their own fleet of Swifts which were every bit as unreliable as London Country's. Thirty-four RTs had been sold back to London Transport in September 1972 to help with shortages, and now London Transport needed every Routemaster they could get hold of either as a source of spares which were still desperately short, or to replace unserviceable Fleetlines on some routes. At first London Transport insisted on London Country bringing them up to the required standard before they would take them, but London Country soon discovered that some were worth more for scrap instead of the expense of repairing them – especially given the huge backlog of other buses awaiting repair and which were actually needed for service. Such was London Transport's need however that they relented and took several RMLs in poor condition, even re-purchasing some which London Country had already sold for scrap. With the influx of many new Nationals which were used to convert the last of the major trunk routes, London Country actually turned a dire shortage of Routemasters into a surplus and they were able to sell over 70 back to London Transport including around 20 that were only fit for spares and scrap.

Despite many previous conversions of busy crew routes to omo the actual conversion day could still prove to be difficult. On 19th November 1977, the 330 and 341 worked jointly between St Albans and Hatfield were converted, and Les Bland, who had joined London Transport as a conductor at St Albans in 1969, recalls the events of that Saturday morning very well. St Albans already had a number of spare conductors from previous reductions on crew working, and on that morning the garage canteen was full of conductors on standby 'to instructions'. On the 330 route, only the section between St Michaels and Leverstock Green was through open country, the rest being a busy interurban route with frequent stops, and the previous 73-minute end to end running time was increased by only seven minutes to account for one-manning. Even as late as November 1977, the 330/341 still provided a ten minute headway out of St Albans through Fleetville and Smallford, so as drivers struggled to come to terms with issuing fares, and on a route with a tight schedule and busy traffic, the situation descended into chaos very quickly. By mid-morning, Les Bland and a number of the other conductors were sent down to St Peters Street to crew the new omo Leyland Nationals. His first journey was to take on a 330 toward Hemel Hempstead, and when the bus left the St Peters Street stop with Les collecting fares, the bus was running so late that it should have just been leaving Hemel Hempstead on its return trip! Les was relieved mid-afternoon by which time buses were beginning to catch up time, but the whole timetable remained chaotic. On the following Monday, conductors were once again rostered in the morning peak to avoid late running and it was several days before the service managed to be run to something approaching the scheduled timetable. The excess of spare conductors at St Albans

Hertford rostered only one bus to the 341, the main allocation always having been run by Hatfield. At the same time as the major conversion of St Albans and Hatfield's crew work on the 330/330A/341 to omo in October 1977, Hertford also received a number of new SNBs to convert the last of their crew workings. In 1976, RMC 1505 waits in Hertford Bus Station for a journey to St Albans, and despite the conversion, Hertford retained unofficial crew working for another two years. (Ian Pringle)

was by no means unique as the one-man conversions gathered pace. Conductors remained rostered to several workings on St Albans omo routes, particularly over the whole length of the 355 from Borehamwood right through to Harpenden, some turns on the 361, and on the former crew routes 391/391A. Money was wasted though on rostering conductors to some of the 365 to Luton, but perhaps the most bizarre crew workings of all were two morning journeys to Hitchin and back on the 304. After the 330/341 conversions, there were still a handful of peak hour crew workings, but as other garages began to lose conductors, shortages had to be covered by borrowing from elsewhere. Tring garage suffered as staff left with closure imminent, and more than once Les Bland and his colleagues were ferried by bus all the way from St Albans to Tring for a duty on the 301, only to be collected and ferried back at the end of the shift! He also worked the 716A from Hatfield all the way to Woking without ever having been over the route and before he finally left, became the pilot for new drivers learning the 727 Green Line route. Les's experiences were by no means unique, and illustrate another hidden cost involved in shedding large numbers of conductors in a few short years.

Among the many new buses arriving in 1977, one of the more unexpected purchases was a batch of ten secondhand 36ft long AEC Reliances from Barton Transport which had cramped three and two seating with narrow gangways. They were purchased to cover newly won – mostly school – contract work from Dorking, and to allow some SMs to be replaced at Leatherhead for use elsewhere where other garages were still suffering shortages from a lack of serviceable SMs. At Leatherhead, their high seating capacity was also useful on the busy 418, and for school journeys, and like all vehicle types at the time, they were soon rostered to a variety of work, Dorking even using them on some 714 Green Line journeys if nothing else was available.

During the vehicle shortage, Leatherhead worked much of the 408 and 470 with the hired Bournemouth Fleetlines, but the appearance of an RN was very rare as they were mainly intended for school contracts. RN 3 is on the stand at Dorking bus station on a 470 to Croydon substituting for one of the Bournemouth Fleetline buses, which could not always be relied on for a full day's work. The lady looks towards the garage, probably waiting for the driver to return. (Alan Charman)

By April 1978, the combined total of new Atlanteans and Nationals in stock had reached 482, a number which was increasing all the time. In addition 67 Bristol LHSs were in service plus the single batch of 15 Bristol VRs at Grays which had been purchased as a stop-gap when they suddenly became available following the cancellation of an order by Bristol Omnibus. The reliability of the fleet had increased measurably as more and more of these had come into service, even allowing the withdrawal and sale of the 45 SMs mentioned earlier. The wholesale process of converting crew operated double deck routes to omo which had begun with the 410 in February 1972 had continued steadily and was accelerated once the worst of the vehicle shortages had been overcome. There were still a number of odd scheduled crew workings mainly during peak hours, but by summer 1978 regular all day crew operation was confined to just seven routes requiring a maximum of 72 Routemasters with all three variants still in service, plus three more RCLs at Grays for peak works journeys. Of the remaining routes, the 347 was the last of what were perhaps the traditional long distance trunk routes which had both busy interurban sections and stretches of open countryside. It was also the last remaining regular crew worked route in the northern part of the network. Of the others, the 403 and 406 were suburban, while the 411 and 477 were less busy with a mix of urban and countryside sections. The urban 480 was the busiest and most frequent, linking Erith and Dartford with Gravesend, while Windsor retained just one RML to work the 407 Slough town service run jointly with Alder Valley.

The Bournemouth Atlanteans were never formally allocated anywhere but Leatherhead, so the use of one by Swanley on the 477 was extremely unusual. Bournemouth 264 is seen at St Mary Cray heading to Dartford on a 477 showing a very clear blind display. (Brian Speller)

Concurrent with the overhaul of the Green Line network, constant changes to the bus routes were being implemented. In October 1972 a small extension had been made to the 384 when it was extended from Letchworth to Baldock. This coincided with the opening of the new Lister Hospital on the northern edge of Stevenage, and extending the 384 was intended to provide a link for visitors from Baldock and Letchworth to the hospital. It had been May 1936 since London Transport had withdrawn from Baldock as part of the changes following the 1933 Act, and London Country's extension only came about because, in 1972, United Counties had insufficient capacity at Hitchin depot and were unable to provide a daily service to link to the new hospital. There were only two evening trips to Baldock to coincide with hospital visiting times, but what was significant was that on Sundays six round trips were provided, bringing a Sunday service to the Letchworth – Stevenage section of the 384 for the first time since the remaining three journeys had been withdrawn at the end of 1966. It had been a worthwhile initiative, but loadings were poor from the beginning, and in January 1977 the extension to Baldock was withdrawn including the Sunday service. Stevenage's operation of the Baldock journeys had been almost entirely with RFs until 1976 when spare RPs and even SMs from the Superbus allocation were used, but RPs and SMs were often unavailable so RF 45 – Stevenage's last RF – continued to be used as well as RF 212, which was borrowed from Hertford for a few days.

In October 1977, United Counties took over the operation of the 383. With a depot in Hitchin, they avoided the dead mileage costs London Country had to incur in running out from Stevenage every day, thus allowing Hertfordshire to reduce its subsidy for the route. At the same time, London Country took over United Counties' route from Hitchin to Welwyn, extending it to Welwyn Garden City. This consisted of a handful of journeys and was all that was left of the once hourly Birch Brothers 203 route to London acquired in 1969 when United Counties had taken over the former Birch bus network.

The 304 was another marginal rural route in Hertfordshire, its timetable having been cut back during the week to a few shopping journeys beyond Whitwell into Hitchin. On Saturday 19th April 1975, BL 7 has left the main road at Chapelfoot and climbs up to St Pauls Walden on the 11.46am 304 from Hitchin a few weeks before the timetable saw something of a revival. Until late 1977, a quirk of crew rostering at St Albans, saw a couple of Monday to Friday journeys to Hitchin and back run with a conductor. (Author)

RPs officially replaced RFs on the 383 at the end of 1976, although their greater length could be difficult on the tight turn in the village on to the stand at Weston. The poor availability of the RPs meant that Stevenage continued to use RFs much of the time well into 1977, but on 21st May 1977 RP 26 has been rostered and has just pulled away from the terminus in Weston on a journey to Hitchin. Three months later, the route was taken over by United Counties, but RP 26 would remain in service until withdrawn and sold early in 1981. The original Holden pattern shelter is still at Weston today. (Mike Harris)

In November 1977, the routes in west Kent centred on Sevenoaks suffered large cuts in a complete revision of the timetables, following on from equally severe cuts in November 1975 which had reduced vehicle requirements sufficiently to remove the hired Royal Blue MW coaches. In March 1978, Maidstone & District had abandoned their rural 68 and 106 routes west of Sevenoaks, and two months earlier had taken over the service round the Troy Town loop in Edenbridge from London Country. The November 1977 cuts took four more buses out of Dunton Green's Monday to Friday allocation and removed most of the evening services. London Country had already taken over some of Maidstone & District's local workings in Gravesend, but in March 1978, they shut their Gravesend depot completely, withdrawing much of the rural mileage. At the same time, London Country took over the remaining local routes, and the trunk 480 route was converted to omo on Sundays when there were enough Leyland Nationals spare from the weekday town service allocations. More significant was the withdrawal of the 401 south of Eynsford through Otford to Sevenoaks. The 401 had provided a long standing link from Dartford to Sevenoaks since pre-war days, and when London Country took over, still ran an hourly service, seven days a week with additional shopping journeys over some sections. Between Otford and Eynsford however was open country, often run with no stops, and like so many other services, the link had long since become unprofitable. Thames Weald provided a skeleton replacement three times a day into Sevenoaks, and London Country ran a limited Sunday service numbered 456 to replace the 401. The 456 was principally intended for visitors to Darenth hospital in Dartford, but was barely used and soon failed. The Bank Holiday 15-minute headway on the 401 through the Darenth Valley that had once run was a very distant memory.

Cuts in services across the whole country had if anything accelerated during 1976 and 1977, and the National Bus Company annual report for 1977 gave no room for optimism that this trend would not continue. Passenger numbers across the whole group had gone down by around 12% over two years, and the only reason total fares revenues had gone up was as a result of swingeing fare increases together with more than £26 million from local authority support for loss making routes. The NBC operating surplus therefore showed a significant increase over 1976, but this was before allowing for capital expenditure for continuing fleet renewals. A large proportion of the cost savings made through service cuts and greater use of buses and staff had been offset by inflation, and NBC made it quite clear that the levels of cost reductions made in 1977 could not be repeated in 1978, emphasising that continuing service cuts were unavoidable without further increases in revenue support.

During 1976, Surrey began looking critically at the escalating costs of supporting not just rural routes across the county, but those in the outer suburbs, the network to the south and west of Kingston being of the most concern where many of these once busy routes could not continue without support. They were all operated by London Transport whose outdated working practices and huge overheads meant that their operational costs per mile were much higher than those of London Country or other operators. London Transport still operated some 25% of bus mileage in Surrey, and routes such as the 206, 215, 218, 219, 224, 237 and 264 were all having to be subsidised, while the gap between commercial receipts and public subsidy was widening. Surrey looked at ways in which this could be contained, since savings could accrue from transferring some routes to London Country. London Transport however had the final veto over any operator wishing

to run a service within the Greater London area as a result of the 1969 Act which had transferred overall responsibility for London Transport to the Greater London Council. Negotiations were therefore complex, but in January 1978, the first change was made when the 237 was cut back to Sunbury village just inside the Surrey boundary. London Country took over the outer end of the 237 to Chertsey, incorporating it into a new 459 route on to Woking, London Transport had withdrawn the 215 beyond Cobham to Ripley at the end of 1966 and this was cut back further to Esher and diverted to Claygate in April 1977 to allow the 206 to be completely withdrawn. The 206 had been the only London Transport route entirely within Surrey, and the latter was unable to continue subsidising it in its current form. The 264 from Kingston to Hersham Green was also withdrawn.

It was only an accident of the 1933 Act that the 224 (Uxbridge – Staines – Laleham) had not been a Country area route, the section south of Colnbrook into Staines being completely rural, running to an hourly headway. South of Colnbrook, the route was little used, and between Wraysbury and Staines had always been paralleled by the 460 from Slough. It was therefore withdrawn, in 1976, although in 1977 the section from Staines to Laleham was covered by just four journeys in the morning only for passengers to a health centre which London Country numbered 451. Surrey initially wanted to retain a link from Poyle to Staines and after the withdrawal of the 224, began a route numbered 467 in January 1977 linking the two, but routed over Stanwell Moor via Yeoveney which even then remained comparatively isolated. There were only six weekday journeys, but these were reduced to Saturdays only in November that year. It was a worthwhile attempt but was withdrawn in 1980.

The changes in north Surrey resulted in London Country taking over parts of former London Transport Central Area suburban routes. The 459 was part of these changes, running between Knaphill through Woking to a new shopping centre at Feltham, and replaced the old 237 between Chertsey and Sunbury village. On 13th July 1979, SM 123 picks up in Chertsey on a 459 journey to Feltham (Mike Harris)

Before London Transport had finally managed to gain agreement for one-man operation of these routes in 1964, Kingston, Norbiton and Fulwell garages had rostered a total of 53 crew operated RFs between them, but the routes had suffered an even steeper decline than many of the Country area routes, and although London Country benefited from the changes, the overall effect was one of further reductions. In addition to the former London Transport workings taken over, Alder Valley also withdrew the last of their journeys on the 48B from Chertsey to Lyne and Longcross. This was a minor rural service which had once been run with Dennis Falcons remotely from Woking depot, so London Country replaced it with a few shopping journeys added to the 462 timetable. All these changes added a few duties to Addlestone garage.

Town services in Welwyn Garden City were completely revised in May 1978, the four main routes being numbered G1–G4 with some through routes being adjusted to cover parts of previous town services. In July, those at Crawley were also revised with a new network branded as 'C Line', operated with mostly new Atlanteans. Amongst these and many other changes in that year, however, three were significant. The last day of crew operation on 347/347A was 31st August, thus bringing to an end daily rostered crew working in the northern area, and a few weeks later RT 604 was finally withdrawn at Chelsham. In May 1977, four RTs had been recertified for a final period of service, and after RT 981 was withdrawn from service at Reigate in February 1978, RT 604 was the last one. It suffered engine failure in September, and plans to repair it were abandoned. Six months later, when London Transport's last RTs were withdrawn from Barking garage, a huge celebration took place with thousands of people turning up on the day to see off the last of these iconic buses, myself among them, but London Country's last one passed by with no ceremony because of its sudden end. My own last journeys on Country RTs had been on RTs 1018 and 3461 in December 1976 on the 403 and I never managed to return again before RT 604 came out of service. RT 1018 would survive as Stevenage's training bus until 1981. Chelsham also had RF 684, the very last unaltered bus RF, and I managed a journey on it to Caterham on the 453 on a dull autumn afternoon in November 1977 – my last journey on a Country bus RF. It lasted a further six months before withdrawal, to be replaced by RF 221 from Northfleet, which ran until November 1978, outlasting RT 604 by a few weeks. RF 221 was therefore the last one used on bus routes and, like RF 684 before it, was generally used on the morning school journeys on the 464, and then a few afternoon trips to Caterham on the 453. These buses too disappeared quietly and without ceremony, unlike their Central area counterparts. The last day of the red RFs, 31st March 1979, coincided with the last day of the 382 route from St Albans to Codicote. Successive timetable cuts had reduced the 382 to just two journeys Monday to Friday, and it had survived probably much longer than could be justified.

The 301/302 were among the first routes to receive new RTs in 1948, running on them for 27 years until replaced by Leyland Nationals in May 1975. On 17th August 1974, nine months before the end, RT 1018 pulls on to the A41 at Two Waters on a 302 to Watford Heath. The bus had been allocated to Hemel Hempstead for more than 11 years before going to Tring where it was delicensed in May 1975 after omo conversions. It was returned to service in 1976 and was one of four final RTs re-certifed in April and May 1977 and repainted into full NBC livery. It went to Chelsham for the 403 until September 1977, finally becoming a training bus and had the distinction of being London Country's last RT when withdrawn from Stevenage in 1981. (Mike Harris)

New Atlanteans allowed improvements to some town service networks, and following the revisions in Welwyn Garden City, Crawley's town services were completely revised and re-branded as 'C Line' in July 1978, underpinning Crawley's operations. AN 149 runs through Pound Hill on one of the works journeys from Manor Royal displaying the C Line logo applied to the town service buses. (Mike Harris)

In March 1979, the whole of the Watford area was re-organised with a new network branded 'Watford Wide', all routes being given numbers with a 'W' prefix in the same way as the 'C Line' routes at Crawley the previous year. This gave a more efficient use of buses, and the overall effect was a small increase in service requiring five more drivers. At first this was a problem since Garston (who had suffered shortages for years) were still short of around 30 drivers, but a new recruitment campaign was successful. While services around Watford itself saw a small improvement, another long established trunk route – the 321 – was withdrawn south of Maple Cross to Uxbridge. This had been a major link with a 30-minute headway, but the section from Maple Cross to Denham was mostly run non-stop with no intermediate passengers, and the faster 724 or 727 Green Line which covered the same road provided an alternative half hourly headway anyway.

In 1977, a small number of buses were repainted to celebrate the Queen's silver jubilee year. AN 41 has arrived at the terminus at Kinsbourne Green just north of Harpenden on one of the many 321 journeys which turned there. The driver has set the incorrect intermediate blind, the one displayed being intended for short journeys between Garston and Rickmansworth. The text refers to the withdrawal of the route south of Maple Cross two years later. ((Ian Pringle)

On 24th April, a major development in revitalising the Green Line network was the introduction of the 747 non-stop express between Heathrow and Gatwick, using the M25 and M23 motorways. This became an extremely successful 'flagship' service, and more than 40 years later still operates, albeit under a different format.

Now that the old boundaries created by the 1933 Act had been broken down, further exchanges of routes were taking place, and in September the long country section on the 339 from Ongar to Brentwood was handed over to Eastern National, reducing London Country's operation to the Harlow – Epping – Ongar part which – even with the rural run into Ongar – was just about profitable because of the greater traffic in and out of Harlow and Epping. At the same time, London Country took over Eastern National's 269 from Grays to Brentwood which they re-numbered 369.

Despite continuing decline in the Surrey Hills routes, London Country made a bold step in September by extending the 412 from Holmbury St Mary to Ewhurst and Cranleigh, creating several new links. Like Tillingbourne a few years earlier, London Country sought to take advantage of Cranleigh as a shopping destination. Indeed, Surrey County Council had encouraged them to extend the route as part of their own review of services in the area, notwithstanding objections from McCann at Forest Green since the 412 now ran over some of the same roads as their route. The extension involved a double run from Holmbury St Mary to Sutton and back, and the five journeys to Cranleigh plus a sixth on Saturday with some additional school journeys and a new peak hour link with Ockley proved initially successful. It was a sign of the times though that the last departure from Dorking to Holmbury and Sutton was at 6.10pm during the week, and even earlier at 5.35pm on Saturdays. At the same time, the 412 Ranmore journeys were withdrawn, but the route was extended instead from Dorking by running along the main A25 towards Reigate before climbing up Pebble Hill to terminate at Boxhill at the same place as the 416 from Leatherhead. The additional service provided two morning shopping journeys into Dorking every day with an additional third journey on Saturday afternoon.

The extension of the 412 to Cranleigh in September 1979 necessitated a double run from Holmbury St Mary to Sutton and back, whilst at the same time three journeys were extended from Dorking to Boxhill. On 12th May 1981, SNB 352 is working the 12.26pm Boxhill to Cranleigh journey and is about to make the tight turn into the lane down to the Volunteer pub at Sutton to reverse. The bus is displaying the wrong blind, one which was used only for the afternoon school journey via Sondes Place School in Dorking. The Cranleigh extension proved shortlived and was withdrawn three months after this picture was taken, after which the 412 reverted to the old terminus here at Sutton, and the three Boxhill journeys were added instead to the 425. (Author)

The Ranmore service was not abandoned completely however, being reduced to just two morning journeys on Tuesday and Friday only which could be run by the spreadover bus from the 425 allocation. The Newdigate service on the 439 was also cut back to a skeleton timetable, arranged so that the lunchtime journey could also be worked by the same bus that worked the Ranmore journeys. In January 1979, Tillingbourne had to withdraw some of their rural mileage into Horsham to reduce losses, one being the service from Colgate village which was instead incorporated into a new 474 route by London Country running from Crawley via Worth Forest and Colgate into Horsham. One unusual outcome of the changes was an evening journey on Tillingbourne's 451 Horsham town service which was run by London Country with a bus from the 414 'on hire' to Tillingbourne, and which became necessary because the Tillingbourne driver would have exceeded his permitted hours by working this journey himself. This cannot have been economic, but represented the sort of operational changes which would become commonplace later when odd journeys on many routes were run under contract to different operators. In March 1979, a rural route in Hertfordshire was acquired when London Country replaced a service from Much Hadham and Hunsdon into Harlow formerly operated by Blue Diamond Coaches. Numbered 354, it was nothing more than a subsidised skeleton shopping service. It was later extended to Bishops Stortford, but to avoid the bus sitting empty waiting for the return shopping journey, it was run back to Harlow via Sawbridgeworth, the journeys being given route number 338. To operate the later return shopping journey from Bishops Stortford on the 354, the bus worked back from Harlow as a 338 to reverse the working, whilst the Saturday service was worked by Hertford from the 350 schedule.

On 28th July 1979, MBS 415 has arrived at Horsham Carfax having worked the 1.54pm from Crawley on the short lived 474 via Colgate, taken over from Tillingbourne after they had withdrawn from the route in January that year. I had travelled on the bus from Crawley, one of my last trips on a 'London Transport' bus. It was Crawley's last MBS and one of the last in service, but would put in another 16 months before withdrawal in October 1980, not long before the last ones of all were withdrawn at Northfleet. (Author)

The 441C ran short journeys from Staines to Englefield Green to supplement the main 441, and was renumbered 442 in November 1977 when it was converted to omo with Nationals, which could not accommodate suffix letters in the three track number blinds. RML 2453 works a journey back to Staines on the route sometime before conversion. Staines retained a few RMLs for another 18 months and this bus would be its last RML until it was sent to Northfleet for the 480 in April 1979. (Ian Pringle)

Vehicle shortages had almost been eliminated by 1979, but Godstone had a problem in January when the Certificates of Fitness of their entire fleet of Fleetline AFs all came due for renewal at the same time. New Atlanteans had arrived towards the end of the previous year to eliminate crew working on the 409/411, but there were insufficient to cover for the AFs while they were away. These buses had been new in February 1972 when they converted the 410, and had spent their whole life since on the route. Although most were recertified and returned to service, Godstone had to borrow whatever was available in the interim, even including what by then were elderly XFs from East Grinstead which did not perform too well on the ascent of Westerham Hill. A couple of RMLs which had been kept back after the conversion of the 409/411 were also put to good use, but these went to Northfleet in the summer where the CoFs of many of its ailing Routemasters began to expire, and operation on the 480 became un-reliable again. Northfleet was reduced to using any available vehicle for the 480, even including the occasional BN – all crew operated – but by November new Atlanteans began to trickle in to take over the route and ease the problem.

Even after successive reductions, Hertford continued to roster a couple of peak hour double deck workings on the 331 and 337 to Buntingford into the 1980s. On a cloudy evening on 31st July 1979, AN 63 is working the 5.46pm 337 from Hertford to Buntingford through open farmland as it passes the Hobbs Lane timing point at Dassels on the road from Braughing. Like the picture of SNB 216 taken three years later, the bus appears completely empty. One can but wonder when was the last time anyone had used this stop which still retains the original LTE flag. (Author)

As the 1970s came to an end, perhaps one of the greatest symbols of the decline in the industry had been the closure of the AEC works at Southall in 1979. This had been what might be thought of as the 'spiritual home' of London Buses for more than 50 years, but British Leyland's relentless drive towards a 'low cost' universal product had slowly sidelined manufacturers like AEC. Bristol suffered the same fate in the drive for standardisation of models which took less and less account of the different operating conditions between intense urban and light rural routes – a factor which had always been London Transport's major achievement in the design of its buses. The Leyland National was reliable and cheap to buy, but actual 'in-service' operating costs were much higher than the models they replaced. Spares were more expensive, they needed more frequent maintenance, and the terrible poor quality seats were easily damaged, requiring constant repair. The decline in Bristol's fortunes had meant they had less and less capacity to provide adequate quantities of spares for LH and VR models which required much more attention than the Lodekkas and MWs of the 1960s, which had been much more reliable and required a minimum of work to keep them on the road.

By the end of 1979 London Country's fleet of Leyland Nationals had reached its final total of 543, by far the largest of any NBC company. 230 Atlanteans were in service, and with the 67 Bristol LHs and 15 Bristol VRs, London Country had just over 850 buses which were not only new but had increased reliability considerably – albeit still not to the extent of the former fleet of RTs, RFs and Routemasters. Ninety of the perennially troublesome SMs had been withdrawn, and half of the equally unreliable RPs were either withdrawn and stored or awaiting sale. In October, Addlestone garage was the last to receive new Nationals after suffering years of trying to maintain service with SMs and RPs so that by the year end there were only four SMs still scheduled there. Small numbers of Merlins were still in use, and the goal of 100% omo had almost been achieved. The new Atlanteans at Northfleet on the 480 remained crew operated, and this, along with the 477 at Swanley and the 403 at Chelsham, were the only remaining all day regular crew duties.

RMC 1471 was the first Routemaster ever operated by Chelsham when it arrived in April 1976, and between March and October the following year, a batch of Maidstone Corporation Atlanteans were sent to Chelsham during the period when their Routemaster fleet was at its most depleted. Not long after they arrived, Maidstone 35 waits at Croydon Bus Station for a 403 to Warlingham Park Hospital while RMC 1471 behind is working one of the few remaining evening peak hour 403 express journeys to Warlingham. (John Bishop)

By the end of the 1970s, Dorking's operations had been much reduced, but at least most of its mixed allocation of types had been replaced with new Nationals which arrived at the end of 1977. SNB 351 was one of these and is laying over at Goodwyns Farm Estate waiting to work a local 449 to Chart Downs. It shows the almost illegible blind display which came from masking the aperture and cramming too much into a small space. (Ian Pringle).

The last years of London Transport's management of its Country Bus Department had been inadequate, perhaps woefully so, and like other operators everywhere, it had made little serious attempt to undertake a fundamental review of the operation. Other than continually reducing frequencies and withdrawing a small number of hopelessly unprofitable rural routes, no real attempt had been made to look critically at the network itself, or to respond sufficiently to the urgent need to push through omo conversions at a much faster rate. The Unions themselves had played a large part in the financial decline through their implacable resistance to change and the protection of jobs which became increasingly less necessary. Government policy over a number of years had limited increases in fares which – not just for London Transport – had limited operator's ability to maintain investment in fleet replacement. The result was that management everywhere did too little too late, and in the case of London Transport, once the political decision had been made in 1968 to separate the Country Area from the principal Central Bus network, no effort was put into it in its last year of ownership. Despite this, in ten years, London Country had been transformed from a failing operation with aged buses and huge losses, into what would become one of NBC's most successful subsidiaries. The fleet had been transformed, the Green Line network saved from almost certain oblivion, and the much altered bus routes reduced to reflect their passengers' needs and the local authority subsidies which were available. It had been a difficult and painful process, not assisted in the first half of the decade by unreliable new buses and the subsequent shortage of spare parts, both of which had been major factors in damaging what little customer confidence remained as the daily service became increasingly unreliable. Many passengers had been alienated and lost forever, but the turnaround of the Green Line network had shown what could be done with a suitably bold and radical approach to wholesale change. London Country had at last achieved stability and could look forward with much more optimism than a few years earlier. Everyone had something to be proud of, but as the Company began its second decade, the Transport Act and Deregulation which followed would bring about fundamental changes to the business and the industry as a whole.

3 MAPs and the Last Conductors

The benefits of the turnaround which had begun in earnest three years earlier were now bearing fruit, and 1980 was a year of continuing change as wholesale improvements in vehicles and the route network continued the consolidation. Apart from the three major MAP schemes referred to later on, Crawley town services were revised and improved in March, and in April those at Stevenage completely revised. The old 800 series and Superbus routes were all replaced with a complete new network marketed as 'Stevenage Bus', new route numbers being prefixed with SB to reflect the success of the Superbus initiative. In May, London Country began operations on no fewer than 13 National Express coach routes for the summer season, involving coaches from six garages. At the end of August Harlow's town services were revised in the same way as Stevenage, the old routes being replaced with a new network marketed as 'Town Bus' with T prefixed route numbers. On the same date, there were extensive revisions to the schedules at Hatfield and St Albans, and in November to the schedules at Northfleet, Dartford, Swanley and Grays.

More changes became necessary with the closure of Hertford bus station in March for the redevelopment of the site, and similarly in May when Commercial Road bus station in Guildford was also closed for the same reason. The start of the summer Green Line schedules saw further improvements, and there were many innovations during the year, some of which are covered in this chapter.

Harlow's town services were re-organised in September 1980 under the 'Town Bus' brand, routes being renumbered with a T prefix. AN 87 waits in Harlow bus station to work a T2 journey to Old Harlow on the revised network. The indistinct route number blind shows T2 Old Road – referring to a section of the former main A11 which once ran through the original Harlow village and which became known as Old Harlow once the new town became established. (Ian Pringle)

The urgent need for conversion to omo had meant that a number of busier trunk routes had been operated with single deckers – mostly Leyland Nationals – but now the large numbers of new double deckers entering service allowed a number of these routes to be converted back to double deck. This in turn released numbers of new Nationals which then began replacing the remaining Merlins inherited from London Transport and newer but unsatisfactory Reliances and Swifts. There were therefore constant reallocations throughout the year with minor timetable and schedule changes.

At the beginning of 1980, the goal of 100% omo set a decade earlier had almost been achieved. Chelsham had started to receive new Atlanteans early in 1979, and some of the 403 had been converted, but like the 477 and 480 it was a piecemeal process as new Atlanteans trickled in slowly. While the main all day 403 service had been converted, conductors were still rostered at peak times and on the 403 Express journeys, which could still be busy. Since these were mostly spreadover workings, time had to be made up on some of these during the day, resulting in some off-peak journeys on the 453 retaining conductors. This had always been a quiet secondary route, and by 1980 a conductor's workload to Caterham and back was minimal. When the few remaining RMCs were at last replaced by new Atlanteans on 16th February, however, some crew duties would continue for a further six months. By late 1979, Northfleet had received enough Atlanteans to begin replacing the Routemasters on the 480. Northfleet's RMLs and RMCs had reached a point where their condition was extremely poor, and coupled with expiring CoFs, their operation had become increasingly difficult and erratic throughout the second half of 1979. The 480 required a peak allocation of 14 RMLs Monday to Friday with only one fewer on Saturday, and frequently there were simply not enough available for service, so that every type was put out at some stage as cover, even BNs. With good loads being carried on what was still one of the network's busiest routes, a crew operated BN was a very inadequate substitute, but might be all that was available on certain days. Arrival of the Atlanteans in November 1979 finally solved the problems, although the entire 480 schedules remained crew worked.

The 710 was started in April 1977 as a limited stop commuter service from Guildford to London running via the Kingston by-Pass and omitting Cobham and Ripley. It only saved 10 minutes on the 715 journey time, but was an early example of the radical approach to changing the Green Line network. RP 89 has arrived in Guildford at one of the temporary stops used while Onslow Street and the new bus station were being developed during 1980. (Ian Pringle)

This photo shows Swanley's crew operation of the 493 Sunday service which finally came to an end in December 1979 when new Atlanteans began to arrive for omo conversion, although crew working on the 477 during the week would continue until March 1980. (Peter Plummer)

In January 1976 Swanley received three AEC Regent Vs from Eastbourne allowing three RMCs to go to Dartford where severe shortages of Routemasters had caused frequent disruption to schedules. They were impressive buses and very popular with crews, despite their manual gearboxes. They stayed for only six months and were used almost exclusively on the 477 between Dartford and Cheslfield. In this picture Eastbourne 49 picks up in Orpington. (Mike Harris)

After this, the 477 was the last half-cab crew-operated route. The 493 Orpington Town service was worked by Dunton Green during the week, but after the last of the Sunday services had been withdrawn on Dunton Green's bus routes in 1969, the 493 Sunday service had gone as well. In a reversal however, five Sunday journeys were reinstated in 1975, crew worked by Swanley off the 477 allocation, and these isolated Sunday journeys were still running at the beginning of 1980, although they had been converted to omo in December 1979 when Swanley received its first new Atlanteans. The last official day of RMC operation on the 477 has been much documented. On 5th March 1980, half-cab crew-operation in the former Country Bus area finally came to an end, but it was by no means the end of crew operation. Even after the Atlanteans had completed these last conversions, conductors remained on the 403, 477, and 480. The last official day of two-man working on the 480 was 26th April, while Windsor retained some peak crew workings on the 407 and 458 until May when service revisions finally removed their last conductors. Chelsham's last conductors remained until 31st August when the whole of the 403, 403 Express and 453 were at last converted to omo, but crew working at Swanley on the 477 would continue into 1981.

At the end of 1979, Windsor's only remaining crew duties were on the 407 between Cippenham and Langley Village, plus odd journeys on the 452/457 to Uxbridge. Of Windsor's last two Routemasters, RML 2348 was withdrawn shortly before Christmas, but RML 2422 which had been displaced from the 480 at Northfleet was sent to Windsor for a few more weeks. It was Windsor's last RML and on 11th February 1980, it waits at Cippenham terminus for a journey to Langley. It has a full set of correct blinds, and its appearance suggests that Windsor's engineering staff had made a special effort to turn out the bus as smartly as possibly. Five days later, these last crew duties were converted to omo with new ANs. (Mike Harris)

In the late 1970s, the NBC had begun what would become a large number of 'Market Analysis Projects' more commonly known as 'MAP schemes', the initiative for which had first come from Midland Red who had instigated comprehensive reviews of various parts of their huge network. The purpose was a fundamental review of route networks in a given area to bring about changes in established routes and timetables in an effort to match route patterns more closely to what the travelling public actually wanted, and at the same time reduce costs through more efficient use of fewer buses. In most cases, the need for this had been glaringly obvious at least a decade earlier, and had the MAP initiatives been started in the late 1960s, some of the worst financial losses and service cuts might have been at least mitigated, although a bureaucratic and overly restrictive licensing system would have made such schemes far more difficult to implement. The territorial nature of the large Tilling and BET operators also meant that such reviews – especially where they crossed company boundaries – were not viewed enthusiastically. In the former London Transport Country Area, the completely inflexible 'Special Area' and LPTA boundaries of 1933 would have made some of the cross-border changes which the new MAP schemes brought about impossible. It does not detract however from the fact that none of the former Tilling and BET concerns, or London Transport, took sufficient initiative to undertake a comprehensive and critical review of their route networks.

From the mid-1970s however the involvement of local authorities seeking to get best value for their subsidies, together with a far more realistic approach by operators, driven almost entirely by the need to cut costs, at last provided the impetus for the development of the MAP schemes. One of the main advantages of the MAPs was that they looked at route networks across a given area, regardless of operator, and having arrived at revisions to routes and timetables, the local authority could negotiate subsidies where necessary with existing operators to run these, or invite other, often smaller, operators to take on some routes since they had a lower cost base and often required less subsidy. The MAP schemes were frequently branded with new logos and timetables, but almost inevitably brought about further cuts, although they did achieve many positive results in introducing new facilities that actually had a demand.

A number of the first batch of Atlanteans were transferred to Godstone in July 1977 to replace its ailing Routemasters and convert the 409/411 to omo. On a bright snowy day with the North Downs in the background, AN 114 comes along the A25 between Godstone and Bletchingley on a 411 to Reigate. Despite the universal imposition of NBC corporate livery by then, many of the earlier ANs retained the original LCBS green. (John Miller)

In general bus routes in the Home Counties had tended to suffer worse than many regions due mainly to the greater affluence and high levels of car ownership of its population, and this was especially true of the western end of London Country's area into Buckinghamshire, Berkshire and West Surrey. Bucks County Council needed to cut subsidies, but both London Country and Alder Valley had reached the point where their existing networks were unsustainable without increased support – indeed in the case of Alder Valley, they were even unable to continue with the reduced network they had at first proposed late in 1979. Fundamental revisions were required, and so it was that on 13th April 1980 the new 'Chilternlink' network began following a complete MAP review across Amersham, High Wycombe and the surrounding area. It is to London Country's credit that they had already taken steps to review their own network over the previous few years, and the introduction of Chilternlink made few significant changes to their existing services. Alder Valley however had been appallingly slow to react to falling traffic for a number of years, and they bore the brunt of what were, for them, swingeing cuts. There were major reductions in evening and Sunday services, and Alder Valley's rural routes out of High Wycombe were decimated, five villages losing their bus services completely. In an illustration of Alder Valley's lack of reaction, they still had a proportion of crew operation at High Wycombe, but this ended completely with the new 'Chilternlink' scheme. London Country took over some of the journeys on the Alder Valley route from Great Missenden to High Wycombe, and some journeys on the 362 were extended on to Marlow in place of some Alder Valley workings. In High Wycombe, London Country's service to Totteridge ceased in favour of Alder Valley and the rural section of route between Beaconsfield and Penn was withdrawn. The once-hourly 455 main road route from High Wycombe to Uxbridge was reduced to a single peak hour journey, and the evening service to Watford on the 336 was withdrawn, but these represented only minor reductions compared to Alder Valley's losses.

After many changes to the rural routes from Amersham and Chesham, the 359 became the route from Amersham via Great Missenden and Lee Common to Chesham in November 1975, running five or six journeys each way. The 'Chilternlink' MAP scheme brought more timetable reductions, the 359 being reduced to a skeleton shopping service two or three times a day. A few days before 'Chilternlink' began, BL 16 has stopped at Swan Bottom on a journey to Amersham via Great Missenden. The cross-roads in the background was the timing point, the main road being the route of the short lived 394D which had once carried on to Kings Ash in 1956/57. BL 16 was delicensed and sold soon after this when spare BNs were transferred from other garages. (Mike Harris)

A few weeks after 'Chilternlink' started, a second MAP network marketed as 'Thamesline' came into operation around the Windsor and Slough areas, although its start was delayed by a 12-day strike by Windsor staff in protest at service cuts and further job losses. Although on the edge of London Country's area, Alder Valley's Slough to Maidenhead corridor was one of their busiest with headways of as little as five or ten minutes, some of the Maidenhead routes also running through Slough as far as Langley Village as part of a joint cross-town service with London Country from an agreement with London Transport in 1966. Alder Valley's proportion of crew operation on these routes with aged Bristol Lodekkas had been too great for far too long, and they had to make serious cuts to this along with their trunk route from Windsor to Maidenhead, together with rural mileage from Maidenhead itself. Once again, London Country was far less affected than Alder Valley, the only complete withdrawal being the remaining Saturday only shopping service on the 467 from Staines to Poyle. The 466 and 469 from Staines to Virginia Water were joined to form a circular route and the long standing 457 from Uxbridge to Slough was extended to Windsor and Staines to form a joint service with the equally long standing 441 to High Wycombe. The revised routes were renumbered 441-444 and the new schedules maintained much the same service as before but with fewer buses.

A few months later on 31st August 1980, the 'Weyfarer' MAP scheme came into operation in north-west Surrey. This scheme covered the area around Guildford, Weybridge and Woking, and in the space of a few months completed what had been a total revision to the whole network of routes on the boundary between what had once been Aldershot & District, Thames Valley and London Transport. These three MAP schemes had also swept away the artificial boundary between the three operators which had remained almost unchanged since 1933. Alder Valley again suffered more significant cuts, particularly from Guildford.

At the same time as the 'Weyfarer' scheme, London Country introduced major changes around Epsom when the long established 418, 419 and 481 were all withdrawn. They were replaced with 476, 478 and 479 covering the former 418 from Kingston to Epsom, then splitting to either Langley Vale or continuing to Great Bookham with alternate journeys operating a double run round Wells Estate to replace the 481, The evening service to Langley Vale and The Wells was withdrawn. The 468 to Chessington was altered to cover the 419 to Brettgrave, although on a much reduced timetable with no evening service. SNB 326 had stopped in Great Bookham village near the end of the 479 having worked one of the journeys via Wells Estate. The LT timber shelter and pre-war concrete stop post are still in place albeit with the universal NBC stop flag. (Ian Pringle)

Some Alder Valley workings were taken over by London Country in the 'Chilternlink' MAP reorganisation, after which some journeys on the 362 from Chesham to High Wycombe were extended to Marlow over the former Alder Valley route 29. Amersham had received 15 new SMs in 1971 to convert all their crew work, including the 362, and Chapter one refers to their inadequate performance. Over the next 8 years, no less than 56 of these buses would pass through Amersham in an unending battle to keep enough on the road. New Leyland Nationals were at last sent to Amersham in 1979 to replace the hapless SMs, and SNB 460 is seen here in Marlow on one of the former Alder Valley workings. The prominent 'Chilternlink' branding gives some relief to the awful all-over NBC green. (Barry Le Jeune)

In the aftermath of these comprehensive changes, Alder Valley found itself with more than 50 surplus buses, although a couple of Bristol FLF crew double deckers still remained in service at Maidenhead. NBC's 'forced marriage' of Aldershot & District and Thames Valley to form Alder Valley had never been a happy match. Aldershot & District had been part of the BET federation of operators, and Thames Valley part of the Tilling group, so they had been very different in their fleet, cultures, and operating methods. Alder Valley's management had never attempted a critical review or cut back crew operation to a sufficient extent, and it was widely believed that in 1980 the Company was close to financial collapse and closure. In the end, it was the savage cuts – to some extent forced upon them by the MAP schemes – which were a significant factor in Alder Valley's survival. It would be interesting to speculate on the consequences of Alder Valley ceasing to trade in terms of what this would have meant to London Country. The corridors from Aylesbury to High Wycombe, and Maidenhead to Windsor and Slough together with the High Wycombe town services, and perhaps the Guildford to Horsham route, would almost certainly have ended up with London Country, greatly increasing their route network.

The 'Weyfarer' scheme did however bring greater cuts to London Country than in the 'Chilternlink' changes, Guildford and Addlestone losing around 25% of their allocation between the two garages. The 462 between Leatherhead and Staines was dramatically cut to just four journeys as far as Chertsey, the previous hourly headway on to Staines being replaced by the extension of an Alder Valley route running to a joint frequency with London Country's 436. Although not part of 'Weyfarer', the Surrey Hills routes had got to the point where some serious changes had to be made. Other than odd peak journeys to Holmwood, the 414 trunk route was cut back to Dorking, the 714 Green Line route being extended to

Horsham in its place, while at the same time being reduced to just six journeys beyond Kingston into London. The circular part of the 439 through Holmwood and Newdigate was drastically cut to just four journeys between Dorking and Newdigate via Leigh, the rural section of the 425 from Redhill and Reigate through Leigh to Dorking being abandoned completely. The previous 439 journeys through Dorking to Guildford were withdrawn, leaving the 425 with only an hourly headway all day. Tillingbourne co-ordinated their 448 timetable to give a 30-minute headway between Guildford and Gomshall, although Tillingbourne's evening service on the 448 was withdrawn, resulting in the last journey from Guildford departing as early as 5.45pm. The long standing 470 trunk route from Croydon to Dorking was completely withdrawn except for a few school journeys between Epsom and Dorking, leaving only an hourly headway between Dorking and Leatherhead on the revised 714 timetable.

During the first half of 1980, London Country came to agreements with the Trade Union on what were termed 'Productivity Schedules'. Running times on many routes were reduced in the evenings and all day Sundays, together with some layover times at termini. Combined with the MAP schemes in the west of the network, and many changes elsewhere, total vehicle requirements were reduced, some of the resultant savings being shared with staff. The savings were extremely worthwhile, 20 fewer buses being required on weekday schedules between six garages in the south and western area, and a further 16 on Sundays between five in the northern area.

In November, further cuts in support by both Surrey and Sussex brought about the withdrawal of the 475 to Handcross, while the 424 East Grinstead–Reigate

The three dual doorway SMWs spent all their time at Crawley, one being used on the 475. The limited service beyond Pease Pottage to Handcross was withdrawn in November 1980, and a few months earlier SMW 1 waits at Northgate to work one of these journeys. It has been repainted into NBC livery, but at least has had the white band applied rather than overall green. The livery makes an interesting comparison to the photograph of SMW 3 in chapter one. (Ian Pringle)

timetable was cut to just seven journeys Monday to Friday and six Saturday. This once important route had been reduced from half hourly to hourly, the Sunday service going with the start of the winter 1967 schedules, but now it was nothing more than a two-hourly daytime shopping service. Once a timetable has been reduced to this level, it represents 'the beginning of the end' since any further reductions leave only a skeletal, irregular timetable which serves little use and deters the remaining passengers, but London Country had little option in the circumstances. The remaining minimal amount of Southdown's rural mileage from East Grinstead was taken over by London Country and incorporated into the 434/473 routes. Southdown had run their infrequent 87 route through Kingscote and Sharpthorne into Ashdown Forest, plus the two-hourly 36 to Brighton, serving Sharpthorne by a different route out of East Grinstead and which had a double run into West Hoathly. Southdown's 87 shared the same road as the 434 and 473 between Kingscote and Saint Hill cross roads along a road which had been the boundary of the 1933 'Special Area', and if the boundary had been slightly further south, the 87 might have been a London Transport route instead. London Country introduced a new 474 route every two hours covering parts of the former Southdown routes, but giving Sharpthorne and West Hoathly new links to Crawley which had never been possible while the old 'Special Area' boundary existed.

In west Kent, London Country began the 457 and 467 from Sevenoaks to Seal and Kemsing, together with some additions on the 421, replacing the last of Maidstone & District's journeys on their local 55 route, reductions which left M&D with just the hourly service on the trunk route from Sevenoaks to Borough Green and Maidstone. In north Kent, the remaining service on the 450 through Betsham and Bean was withdrawn, the service being revised to an hourly headway between Dartford and a new housing development in Bean. This left Betsham with no service, so one journey in each direction on the 489/490 from Longfield was diverted through the village. Despite some narrow roads at Southfleet (which had once been restricted to GS operation), the routes were then approved for SNBs, but Northfleet had to retain a BN for the single track lane between Westwood and Betsham which was not approved for Nationals.

The major development in 1980 however was the new Transport Act, which received Royal Assent on 30th June 1980, and became law three months later. It brought about what would become a seismic change to the industry, its principal objective being to de-regulate express coach services. The original 1930 Act had differentiated between Stage and Express services by means of a minimum fare, but 'Express' services were now re-defined as services which conveyed passengers a minimum of 30 miles in a straight line. For stage services, the major change was a relaxation on the strict control of fares which allowed operators to pass on increases in costs without the old, and time consuming, process of applying to the Traffic Commissioners for fare increases. Equally, the relaxation allowed operators to reduce fares to undercut a competitor, thereby introducing true commercial competition. For applications for new routes, the balance of proof changed.

Whereas historically, the Traffic Commissioners were required to take account of any objections to an application for a new service, the balance now changed so that the presumption was that the commissioners *'shall grant the licence unless they are satisfied that to do so would be against the interests of the public'*. The interpretation of this very subjective test was left to the Traffic Commissioners, who also

were required to take account of an area as a whole (as opposed to the benefits or otherwise of an individual route) including '*particular communities in the area*', and '*any transport policies or plans which have been made by the local authorities concerned and which have been drawn to the commissioners' attention by those authorities*'. This had the effect of affording district and county councils the opportunity to apply political pressure on the Commissioners to adopt specific policies when considering applications for new routes. Relaxation of fare regulation also meant that the more an operator passed its increased costs on to passengers by increasing fares, the less pressure there would be on local authority subsidies. The real effect of this of course was to save an amount of public funding by passing the costs on to the travelling public with – predictably – further losses in passenger numbers from the many heavy fare increases which came about.

In the following year or so, operators everywhere sought to take advantage of opportunities to start new express coach routes. London Country took early advantage of the new freedoms, and a new London to Guildford commuter route numbered 740 began on 1st September, serving many of the housing areas around Guildford to give a direct link to London. In November the 711 route from Harlow via the M11 motorway to the Central Line at Redbridge began, as did the 736/738 from Watford, Hatfield and Welwyn Garden City to Milton Keynes. The major new route however was the 757 from Luton Airport via the M1 non-stop to London. It ran every hour, seven days a week, and was exactly the sort of innovation the 1980 Act was intended to promote. Less successful was a new 750 route running from Gravesend via Bromley and New Addington to Gatwick and Crawley, started in April before the Act came into effect. With six journeys each way, this was a worthwhile venture, but despite much advertising, and the new links to Gatwick, it did not attract as many passengers as hoped and lasted a little over a year before being withdrawn in June 1981.

Less important changes in the continuing revival of the Green Line network saw the peak hour journeys on the 729 to Wrotham transferred in June to Maidstone and District who could operate the service much more efficiently from Borough Green garage. The remaining southern section of the 716 from London to Woking was paralleled as far as Kingston by the 714, and passenger numbers had long since fallen below a worthwhile level. It was therefore withdrawn completely in April, the section from Hampton Court to Woking, which carried reasonable numbers, being replaced by diverting the 725. Windsor had struggled for some time to operate its full Green Line schedules because of persistent staff shortages, so the reduction of eight daily duties from Windsor's 725 schedules assisted in maintaining the rest of their Green Line work. Addlestone's former 716 duties simply transferred to the 725. Earlier in February, changes in schedules combined with more new coaches had formally removed the last remaining RPs from Green Line routes as well as all but two last SNCs at Dorking for the 714.

Successive service cuts throughout London Country's network had – by 1980 – turned a shortage of vehicles only four or five years earlier into a surplus, and it is worth noting the reduction in the scheduled run-out. London Country had made the first serious service cuts in 1971 with the withdrawal of a few rural routes, and prior to this, the maximum scheduled requirement had been 883 buses and 214 coaches, of which 556 were crew worked. In the intervening period, every route – including the main trunk routes – had been reduced, or in many cases had been completely withdrawn, so that by late 1984 the maximum scheduled requirement had been reduced to 670 buses and 206 coaches, all of which were one-man operated. More than 80 of the coaches were used on routes or contracts which had not existed a decade earlier, further illustrating the effect of the turnaround in the Green Line network. The reduction of around 25% in the number of buses scheduled speaks for itself in terms of the remaining route network.

The 740 was another Green Line innovation introduced in May 1980 as a fast commuter link from Guildford's surrounding estates to London. Two years later it became an all-day service jointly with Alder Valley to Guildford and Farnham, also retaining the peak hour commuter journeys. In July 1982, RS 113 picks up at Hyde Park Corner with a good load on a journey to Farnham. (Mike Harris)

At the beginning of 1980, only 78 buses which had been transferred from London Transport on 1st January 1970 still remained in stock, the handful of Routemasters soon going, as mentioned at the beginning of the chapter. Dorking's last MBs went in February, Crawley's last MBS lasted until November, and East Grinstead's XFs went one by one as their CoFs expired, or mechanical failure rendered them uneconomic to repair. One last former London Transport RT – RT 1018 – remained in stock and a notable event was its withdrawal, having survived as a training bus after its last spells in service at Reigate and Chelsham. It was finally stood down from Stevenage in April 1981, but even after withdrawal, was stored for a few more months until sold off in September. RT 1563 still remained on the fleet, but abandoned and cannibalised at Chelsham where it was used at odd times as a store. Whilst the remaining former London Transport vehicles were almost all phased out during 1980, more surprising was the withdrawal of much newer buses. The one-off batch of Bristol VRs which had been diverted from Bristol Omnibus in early 1977 were all sold to Bristol where they were put to work on Bath City services. London Country had taken them as a short term solution to the slow delivery of Atlanteans, and they had spent their whole 3½ year service life at Grays where they had mostly run the busy 370 route from

Romford to Grays and Tilbury. As the year progressed, a start was made on withdrawing a few of the early dual-door long Leyland Nationals which, although only seven years old, were never completely successful on town services. The requirement for the small BL/BN buses had reduced, and during the year the CoFs of the 1973 BLs expired. In August they had been withdrawn from St Albans and Amersham, being replaced by BNs from southern area garages such as Leatherhead, Dorking and Northfleet where reductions had rendered them surplus. Less surprising was the phasing out of the remaining hapless SMs, only 38 of the original 138 being scattered around the fleet at the start of the year. Service changes and the delivery of new vehicles during the year enabled their gradual withdrawal, so that by the year end there were just five SMs still running – two at St Albans and three at Addlestone. In December, formal operation of Northfleet's last SMAs ceased: no doubt the engineering staff there were glad to be rid of them as were those at Crawley when their three SMWs were replaced in January 1981.

1980 had seen significant change and many new initiatives, the financial benefits of which resulted in London Country making an operating profit for the year. Interest costs on the enormous capital debts turned this into a loss of £334,000, but when one considers that only five years earlier more than £450,000 had been lost just on Green Line routes, then the extent of the turnaround can be appreciated.

London Transport had proposed extending the 390 from Sawbridgeworth to Lower Sheering in the mid 1960s. The extension never happened and it was not until November 1977 that route 391 was begun, replacing the 390 between Harlow and Sawbridgeworth, continuing to Lower Sheering. It was renumbered 338, and on 26th August 1980, BN 35 has arrived in the village from Harlow. There were only four journeys, and Lower Sheering was abandoned in 1983. BN 35 was withdrawn soon after this picture was taken. (Mike Harris)

Whilst London Country's results had shown great improvement, NBC's report for 1980 did not make encouraging reading. In 1979, interest costs on all the capital borrowed to renew fleets had turned a profit of just over £5 million into a loss of almost £12 million. Passenger numbers were still falling at an alarming rate, and overall were about 8% lower in 1980 than the previous year. Of even more concern was that the decline had accelerated sharply in the second half of 1980 to more than 10%. NBC calculated that these reductions had cost about £35million in lost fare revenue. Almost nine million miles had been cut from bus route mileage operated, and the report predicted a similar reduction again in 1981. In only four years NBC's total fleet had been reduced by 20% and staff by about 15%, such that the costs of staff redundancies in 1980 alone had been £5 million. The report concluded by stating that the general service patterns which operated for around 16 hours a day were no longer sustainable, even with the then levels of public subsidy, and that services would have to be cut to around ten or twelve hours a day with further cuts to what few evening and Sunday services still remained. The Government had announced that the Bus Grant would be phased out and, in response, NBC introduced different criteria to extend the service life of buses. Leyland Nationals would have their life extended from 12 to 16 years, with double deckers from 12 to 14 years, and service intervals together with time spent on maintenance would be more tightly regulated. This was perfectly sensible in principle but assumed a greater level of reliability of the buses and availability of spares than was often the case. Given British Leyland's record for often appalling quality and reliability at the time, it also proved to be over-optimistic.

In April 1981 several newer buses were withdrawn when the last SMs and SMWs at St Albans, SMs at Addlestone and the remaining BNs at Hertford were all taken out of service. More notably, the last regular crew operation was finally converted to omo when Swanley's last crew workings on the 477 came to an end. Even after this however, there were still a handful of conductors seeing out their time before retirement, and the rail strike in July 1982 threw up some odd workings with conductors helping out on some reliefs put on to carry additional passengers. RMC 4, which was by then London Country's 'showbus', even saw service at Dorking (where it was kept) on the 714 during the rail strike, and earlier, had been used for a day's work by Garston on the 719 to mark the retirement of its last conductor.

In April 1981, more Green Line changes were introduced, continuing the innovative approach to new routes. Eastern Counties' long established London to Cambridge coach service was replaced by a new jointly operated Green Line route numbered 798, running every two hours to a regular timetable. The old coach service required all passengers to pre-book which, by 1981, was an anachronism and disincentive to many passengers, so that the new regular timetable which operated as a limited stop pay-as-you-enter service was much more attractive. The 798 replaced the 735 between London and Ware, the short leg into Hertford being withdrawn. More innovative still was the new two-hourly 797 route which ran from London to Stevenage, then via Baldock to Royston where it joined the 798 and ran to a joint hourly headway to Cambridge. This in turn allowed Eastern Counties to withdraw all but odd peak journeys on the long-established Royston to Cambridge 145/146 bus route. Later, London Country added some additional commuter and shopping journeys from Letchworth and Stevenage's housing estates to London numbered 794 and 796 to supplement the 797. The new routes were operated by Stevenage, Hertford and Eastern Counties' Cambridge depot and proved very successful. The original 716/716A from Hitchin and Stevenage to London had been replaced by the hourly 722/732 in January 1978 cutting out many stops and adding Brent Cross, so with the introduction of the 797, these were reduced to two-hourly as the 'stopping service' while the 797 ran down the A1 non-stop from Stevenage to Hatfield, then non-stop again to north London, cutting 45 minutes from the 722/732 timetable. The fast 797 service soon rendered the slower route into London superfluous, and in another example of London Country's innovative approach, in November 1982, the service was restored to hourly between Hitchin and Hatfield but with alternate journeys to either Brent Cross or St Albans and Watford. This latter gave much more profitable links, and augmented the successful 724 service between Hatfield and Watford.

At the same time that the new London to Cambridge Green Line route started, another minor, but important change came about as the old 'Special Area' boundaries continued to be broken down. When London Transport had acquired People's Motor Services of Ware in November 1933, one of the routes inherited had been the Hertford to Royston service which ran via Braughing, Buntingford and the main A10 to Royston. Buntingford however, was on the LPTA boundary, so in August 1935, London Transport cut the route back to Buntingford, while Eastern National took over the section northwards from there to Royston. This severed the through facility at the time and was a perfect illustration of the disadvantages of the rigid boundaries which came from the 1933 Act. After United Counties took over Eastern National's Midland Area, their 188 route from Biggleswade to

Royston ran on to Buntingford on Wednesdays and Saturdays. Eastern Counties could have run the Buntingford journeys more economically from their Royston outstation, but this was also outside their territory, and even though both companies were part of the Tilling group, boundaries were often strictly adhered to. This impractical and uneconomic arrangement ran unchanged for 30 years after the war, but the remoteness of the Royston to Buntingford leg from United Counties' depot at Biggleswade meant that by 1980, it could no longer support the losses and gave notice that they intended to withdraw it. London Country agreed to operate one subsidised return journey into Royston and back on Wednesday only, retaining the 188 route number and so from 29th April 1981 returned to Royston 45 years after London Transport had withdrawn. Over time, the Royston service was improved and the 331 extended from Buntingford to provide several through journeys from Hertford and Ware to Royston, giving much improved facilities for villages along the way and restoring the route of 50 years earlier.

With the customary cloud of exhaust, SNB 216 turns out on to the main road at Hare Street working the 7.35pm 337 Buntingford to Hertford on 25th August 1982. Most notable is that the bus is completely empty and it is very unlikely that more than two or three will be picked up all the way back. The later extension of the route to Royston described in the text was a major factor in saving it from complete withdrawal. (Author)

By 1977, operation of the 313 was officially SNB, but any bus would be used where available. The standee layout of MBSs was not popular with passengers or drivers on longer 'country' routes, but their use was often necessary if insufficient SNBs were available. On 7th June 1977, MBS 402 is on one of the extended 313 summer journey to Whipsnade Zoo, and has just passed the cross roads on Whipsnade Heath at the point where the former 337 route crossed the main road on the way to Dunstable. (Mike Harris)

In rural Hertfordshire, there were a couple of new initiatives. On 25th July 1981, London Country and United Counties began a new jointly operated route between Stevenage and Luton running via Knebworth, Codicote and Peter's Green over some of the roads which had once been part of Birch Brothers 205 route, and much later the short lived 365 which London Country had run until shortly before Luton garage closed. As mentioned in the previous chapter, United Counties had taken over the 365 at the end of 1976, and extending it into Stevenage had the benefit of a large town at each end. It ran through very sparse country-side, but its links to these two towns were an attraction for shopping. The route also restored a service to Nup End which London Country had abandoned a decade before in its first round of rural service cuts. Equally notable was that the route was numbered 44, a spare number in United Counties's sequence, rather than in the traditional 300 series from London Transport days. One bus from each end worked a few shopping journeys, London Country's official Stevenage allocation being RP while United Counties generally used a Bristol RE. Initially running only three days per week, the route became successful enough to run four or five journeys a day six days a week, and represented an initiative which would never have been possible a few years earlier.

The 384 between Stevenage and Hertford, one of the most infrequent of the surviving rural routes, remained worthwhile with its then level of subsidy despite decreasing passenger numbers. In November 1981, Hertfordshire County Council agreed to part subsidise a 50% cut in fares on the route as an experiment to see if additional passengers might be encouraged to use it. Although all evening and Sunday journeys had gone, and the daytime service had been reduced to just five journeys each way, a relatively small number of extra passengers would have probably justified the experiment. The 350 and 351 between Hertford and Bishops Stortford still enjoyed an hourly headway with slightly more passengers during the day, and these were also included in the experiment. Sadly – but perhaps predictably – the initiative was unsuccessful and ceased after the three month trial period. By this time, Hertford's overall allocation of buses to its rural routes had been reduced to only 12 with a few odd journeys being interworked from the remaining allocation on the more important routes. The Cuffley service was down to only four journeys, the last bus on the 390 to Stevenage was before 6.00pm and the last on the 331 to Buntingford at 7.20pm, with only one later journey as far as Standon on Saturdays. In other parts of Hertfordshire, the last 304 from St Albans to Hitchin departed just after 5.30pm with only one later journey to Kimpton just before 7.00pm, although even this did not run on Saturdays. Attempts to encourage more usage of the 317 into Berkhamsted on Saturdays referred to in the previous chapter had not been successful and the timetable was cut back. On Monday to Friday there were only four journeys to Berkhamsted and five back, while the Saturday service to Berkhamsted was abandoned altogether, the remainder being reduced to just five journeys which ran only as far as Hudnall Common, leaving even Little Gaddesden without a Saturday service.

The new Hertford bus station opened on 1st August, and required a number of timetable and scheduling changes. The problem with the new facility was the lack of space when compared to the old bus station which had plenty of space for buses to set down on arrival and be parked up without the need for constant empty runs to and from the garage at Fairfax Road. The new bus station had only six stands, each with sufficient room for only one bus, so that only short layovers were possible, and timetables had to be adjusted so that the number of buses at any one time did not cause congestion, since at each end of the stands was an entrance to a new multi-storey car park which needed to be kept clear.

In Surrey, Tillingbourne continued to look at how they might expand their network, and take over some of London Country's routes. London Country's extension of the 412 from Sutton to Ewhurst and Cranleigh which had begun in September 1979 had proved unsuccessful and was withdrawn in August 1981. The Ewhurst to Cranleigh section was adequately covered by other routes, but Forest Green lost its link to Cranleigh with the withdrawal of the 412. In November, Tillingbourne put proposals to Surrey County Council suggesting that they could save around £20,000 per annum in subsidies if they took over the 412 and 425. London Country – understandably – had no wish to lose these routes since by then, Dorking garage's run-out was down to only 15 buses with a further two for contract works, and probably below a level which justified its continuing operation. The loss of the 412 and 425 would have perhaps proved terminal, and although Tillingbourne's proposals came to nothing at the time, they did set in motion a sequence of events which would eventually lead to them taking over London Country's routes, and later still to the final closure of Dorking garage.

New Year's Eve 1981 saw the final closure of East Grinstead garage and the last XF. Although not entirely reliable, the XFs had completed a full service life in their 16 years at East Grinstead, but by 1981 only XF 3 was still running. Mechanical failures and the expiry of Certificates of Fitness had seen the remainder withdrawn. The withdrawal of the 719 Green Line route had cut back East Grinstead's run out to just 13 buses so that the garage had been reduced to little more than an outstation. Passenger loadings on the routes out via Felcourt to Lingfield and to Dormansland and Edenbridge had fallen below any economic level, even with subsidies, so that closure was inevitable. Two decades earlier, London Transport, Southdown and Maidstone & District had more than 30 buses

The three XFs which were sent to Stevenage to start the 'Blue Arrow' routes were replaced by three XA'a from the central area. When London Transport sold all the XAs to Hong Kong in 1974, the three with London Country at East Grinstead were included. Three Atlanteans were ordered to replace them, and had dual door bodies to the standard 'provincial' design then favoured by most NBC fleets. AN 122 stands in rural surroundings outside the Plough at Dormansland on the 428, another route which would disappear among the many changes which followed the closure of East Grinstead garage. (Ian Pringle)

garaged in the town between them, but from 1st January 1982, all were gone. In the route revisions that followed East Grinstead's closure, Crawley and Godstone acquired some additional work, widespread reallocations being part of a major reorganisation, whilst the town itself was left with a bare minimum of services. The last departure to Croydon was at 5.20pm with two more as far as Godstone, and only five journeys remained of the once half hourly service via Felcourt to Lingfield. Reigate took over what remained of the 424, where the last departure from East Grinstead was at 6.30pm on Monday to Friday but as early as 5.30pm Saturday once the shops had shut. The last departure to Crawley on the 434 was at 6.40pm, with one other late journey at 10.36pm. One small compensation was a new 438 which ran from East Grinstead to Horsham along the more direct route via Felbridge and Copthorne, but this service also finished soon after 7.00pm every evening. East Surrey had first served Edenbridge in 1921, but the complete withdrawal of the 485 ended 60 years of an unbroken link to East Grinstead. Maidstone & District introduced a shopping service two days a week but was scant replacement for the hourly headway which had operated continuously since the War. London Country's only remaining Sunday service in the town was five journeys to Crawley and Horsham on the 434 with an infrequent headway every two hours and forty minutes, scheduled so the timetable could be worked by just one bus. Such a timetable, apart from being so infrequent, was impossible to memorise, and did nothing whatsoever to encourage the negligible remaining passengers to use the service. Maidstone & District's route to Forest Row, Hartfield and Tunbridge Wells remained running hourly all day, with the last departure at 10.40pm, even retaining six Sunday journeys, and the infrequent 235 to Edenbridge via Cowden retained four or five journeys a day. During the week, after 6.00pm, there were only 11 further departures combined on all routes out of East Grinstead, only nine on Saturdays, and once again illustrate just how much timetables had been cut in response to declining traffic and increasing losses in what had once been an important country town where the three companies had run 14 different routes between them.

An indirect consequence of the reallocations which occurred following East Grinstead's closure was the withdrawal of the last SMAs from service. Additional work at Godstone also led to Dunton Green being allocated workings on the 410 between Bromley and Westerham for the first time in the long history of the route.

Despite declining bus route mileage in 1981, many more Green Line routes were introduced during the year. The summer only routes to the South Coast – most running just a single return journey one or two days a week – had proved very successful, so much so that they were often run with double deckers and even duplicated on the sunniest days in school holidays. A new 720 Gravesend to London non-stop commuter route started in November, and was so successful that after only a few weeks it required 14 coaches, and within six months had more commuter journeys and a regular daytime service added. In January a commuter route numbered 760/761 was started from housing areas around Crawley to run non-stop via the M23 to West Croydon, the timetable including journeys during the day timed to allow a day in central London by train from Croydon, or shopping in Croydon itself. Six months later, in June, both were withdrawn along with the unsuccessful 750, to be replaced with the 755 which gave better facilities to Croydon. In July, London Transport had withdrawn the mostly rural 247 route from Epping to Romford which itself had replaced the long standing 250 a few years earlier. But for pre-war boundaries between the old Central and Country Bus areas, this might instead have been a Country area route operated by Epping garage, and was one of the most rural of all London Transport's Central Bus routes on the very edge of its network. The 712 Green Line route from Harlow to Romford was diverted to cover the 247, retaining the hourly headway, and adding a few passengers to London Country's loadings. More important however, following the success of the 757 from Luton Airport, was the start of the 767 to Heathrow in January and the 777 to Gatwick in March. Both ran non-stop from London and were marketed as 'Flightline'. At the same time as the 777 began, the frequency on the 757 was doubled to half hourly, more journeys were added to the 747 Heathrow–Gatwick route, and a new commuter and shopping route from Aylesbury through Missenden and Amersham to London was introduced, adding more Green Line work to Amersham on top of the increasing allocation to the London to Oxford routes. The 750 from Watford to Bristol via Reading and the 760 from Heathrow to Northampton via Hemel Hempstead and Milton Keynes began in March and were run jointly with other operators. In May, Southdown's long standing trunk route 23 from Crawley to Brighton was replaced with a faster route run jointly with London Country as Green Line 773, running from Gatwick to Brighton and Hove and successfully marketed as 'Sealine'. Conversely a new 721 commuter service from Dartford to London – following the success of the service from Gravesend – was a complete failure, lasting only five weeks. Its introduction made good sense, but for some reason passengers were simply not attracted to it, possibly because Dartford was closer to London than Gravesend and had a quicker train service. In June, the London to Cambridge routes saw the addition of the 799 via Harlow, Bishops Stortford and Saffron Walden run jointly every two hours by Eastern Counties and London Country from Harlow.

All these new routes which followed from the radical revision of the traditional Green Line network, and were mostly enabled by the 1980 Transport Act, brought about a significant increase in business and profit for London Country, the total Green Line allocation having increased from 135 to 167 in only two years. During the year, 30 new Leyland Leopards with either Plaxton (PL) or Duple (DL) bodies had been received, and further enhanced the Green Line image.

The 760/761 were introduced in January 1981 as part of Green Line's continuing turnaround. They were designed to link Crawley's residential areas to Croydon for shopping trips or for days in London by train from Croydon and there were three journeys each weekday which could be run by one coach. The routes ran non-stop up the M23 and fares were set at about 60% of the parallel rail fare. PL 21 waits in Crawley bus station for a 761 to Croydon. (Ian Pringle)

The 757 had been the first express coach route introduced by London Country immediately following deregulation in 1980. It was an instant success, the hourly headway being later doubled to meet the greater demand, and as this increased further, the double deck Olympian coaches were an obvious choice. In June 1986, LRC 10 runs down Finchley Road into London from Luton Airport. (Mike Harris)

NBC's annual report for 1981 was much better in terms of financial performance, but this had only been achieved as a result of savage cost cuts by reducing the fleet size and a further 9% reduction on overall staff numbers. In his introduction, the Chairman noted that the countrywide cuts in 1981 were the equivalent of taking out an entire 1,000-strong vehicle fleet, staff, and route network – an operation larger than the size of London Country by that time. During the year, overall passenger levels had fallen a further 8.5% compared with 1980, and the enormous cuts in vehicles, staff and premises illustrated the extent to which bus travel continued to fall away. Public revenue support was now well established, but the House of Commons Select Transport Committee had heard evidence as to the dire financial position of many NBC subsidiaries.

London Country however was one of the more fortunate as a result of the realistic attitude to revenue support from most of the Local Authorities in its area, but the early months of 1981 revealed the precarious financial position of many other NBC subsidiaries. In the South East, one of the most critical was Maidstone & District, whose operations in north Kent bordered London Country. So severe were Maidstone & District's problems that they were forced to close their Maidstone headquarters, central works, and Maidstone depot, transferring central works to East Kent at Canterbury as well as closing two other large garages. London Country's Gravesend and Dartford area remained profitable, although major revisions in November 1980 had seen more service reductions, but – like Maidstone & District – their routes elsewhere in Kent remained an increasing burden even with higher levels of subsidy. In April 1981, there were severe cuts to the Sevenoaks and Orpington routes, perhaps one which illustrated the situation best being the diversion of the Tunbridge Wells to London Green Line route off the main road through Weald Village to cover the withdrawal of almost the whole of the 454 timetable, which had served Weald since pre-war days but was reduced to a few odd school and works journeys. The hourly service to Shoreham Village had been an over-provision for some time, and was cut back to an irregular service with just a handful of journeys. The last works services to Fort Halstead and the few remaining journeys on the 402 went at the same time, whilst the main road down River Hill from Sevenoaks to Hildenborough was left with just a skeleton peak hour service. In practice, there were few stops on this section, so few if any passengers were inconvenienced, but the five or six journeys an hour which had once covered this road had carried good loads in and out of Sevenoaks and Tonbridge. By 1980 though, passenger numbers had declined so much that one regular hourly journey was all that could be justified, and this needed to run via Weald Village to serve the few passengers who lived there.

The significant timetable cuts at Sevenoaks resulted in single deckers being unable to cope with full loads on some peak and school journeys so a number of ANs were sent to Dunton Green, after a gap of nine years, to provide more capacity. Cross-scheduling resulted in Atlanteans rostered to work some 404 journeys to Shoreham village. BLs had replaced RFs in 1973 on the 404, in turn being replaced by some SNB workings in 1977. There were some difficulties in running SNBs along the narrow lane into Shoreham with increasing numbers of parked cars in the village itself, but double-deck working at first proved impossible due to a large overhanging tree along the route. Although this was soon resolved, Dunton Green had to use a BN to duplicate the SNB on the journey which carried school children. Double deck operation on the route was far from ideal and did not last long.

The text refers to the return of double deckers to Dunton Green in April 1981 to increase capacity on some journeys after the severe service cuts around Sevenoaks. AN 69 is turning from Shoreham Lane towards Twitton on a 404 returning to Sevenoaks and illustrates the rural surroundings on the route. The road from Shoreham was very narrow in places and made double deck operation difficult. (Peter Horner)

After a year, the effects of the 1980 Transport Act were still the subject of much debate. Politically of course, Norman Fowler, the then Transport Minister, sought to emphasize the benefits of the Act, and there was no doubt that express coach services had been transformed with around 100 new routes having been started in the first year, around 25% of these by National Express. Deregulation was intended to encourage competition, and British Coachways was formed by a consortium of eight independent operators who were all established and well known coach companies to compete on long distance routes. Some such as Grey Green, Parks of Hamilton, and Excelsior of Bournemouth already operated long standing express coach routes, while others such as Shearings and Wallace Arnold had built their reputation on holiday travel. Barton Transport operated both bus services and coach routes. The consortium started operations on 'Deregulation Day', 6th October 1980, on a number of routes in direct competition with National Express, accompanied by dramatically lower fares. Predictably, National Express soon countered this with equal cuts to fares, greatly diminishing the attractiveness of British Coachways' services. From the beginning, it had suffered from a major disadvantage in that they could not achieve the economy of scale of National Express, and were crucially denied access to major interchange points and termini such as Digbeth in Birmingham and Victoria Coach Station in London. Although the operation just broke even, they failed to exceed the average 50% loading they needed to make a profit, with the result that routes were cut back, and fares increased to a level which was commercially viable. One by one, the constituent operators pulled out of the consortium, and when access to Kings Cross coach station in London was suddenly terminated in October 1982, British Coachways ceased operations after only little more than two years. Theirs was not the only failure, and competition proved too great for many smaller operators, but what such failures did achieve was to have the effect of making National Express more innovative and competitive. Indeed passenger numbers at Victoria Coach Station had roughly doubled in the first year of deregulation as a result of the increase in frequent cheap coach routes, a trend which would continue, greatly benefiting the public.

London Country were more fortunate than many because their operating area included a number of large towns within commuting distance of London, and three major airports. The Act therefore provided the opportunity to start a whole network of shorter regional express routes on which good passenger loadings could largely be guaranteed.

The bigger controversy though was the effect of the Act on bus services. The relaxation on control of fares had allowed many innovations such as cheap returns, off peak fares, day tickets, flat fares and weekly/monthly tickets, all of which had helped to encourage extra passengers, although with greatly differing degrees of success. The problem came with rural services where there were few if any additional passengers to attract regardless of innovations in fares, and in a small way, London Country's experiment on the 350, 351 and 384 routes had shown this to be the case. Whilst fares could be reduced to compete with another operator along a given route, or in an effort to attract more passengers, it by no means guaranteed additional income.

Those critical of the Act suggested that competition by lowering fares on profitable routes to attract additional passengers might in reality abstract profit to the extent that an operator could no longer support its rural services without yet more subsidy. The Government however, encouraged by the success of the deregulation of express coach services, considered a similar deregulation of bus services. Two trial areas were set up – in Devon and Cumbria – to test how this might work, and to allow any operators to challenge existing ones in competition on existing routes where they felt they could be operated commercially or with less subsidy. Critics were concerned that this could give rise to a situation where a 'new' operator could begin running over another operator's existing profitable route which would abstract traffic, and reduce the original operator's ability to support its loss making routes. Traffic Commissioners did retain the power to protect the public from a monopoly position where the sole operator on a route might raise fares to an unreasonable level, and – importantly – they could also regulate the terms of competition where they perceived it might be prejudicial to the cross-subsidisation of rural services.

AN 24 was another of the double deckers transferred to Dunton Green in 1981, to increase capacity on some routes. They were used on much of Dunton Green's share of the 483, and the bus is coming along the road from Botley Hill on the top of the North Downs before the double run into Tatsfield and the long descent down to Westerham.
(Peter Horner)

Just such a situation arose in Cumbria where Yeowarts, an independent operator from Workington, applied to run along the main Workington to Whitehaven route together with some Whitehaven town services. These routes provided the bulk of Cumberland's revenue and profit, from which they subsidised most of the remainder of their network, several of which routes served isolated Lakeland valleys and hamlets. Cumberland objected on the basis that Yeowart's routes would prejudice their ability to maintain the rural routes, and was therefore against the public interest. The Traffic Commissioners agreed, but Yeowarts appealed. It was noted at the time that no appeal had ever been refused under the old 1930 Act, and after a long and protracted process, the appeal was decided in favour of Yeowarts who won most of what they wanted. Cumberland responded by abandoning much rural mileage, the routes from Cockermouth to Buttermere and the once weekly route to Wasdale – undoubtedly two of the most isolated rural routes in the country – being among them. The public outcry which followed what became known as *'the Yeowarts fiasco'*, gave much credence to those who saw the 1980 Act as the beginning of the end for rural bus routes. In reality however, competition was mostly limited, there being an understandable reluctance among established operators to challenge the status quo, and the Yeowart's case largely proved to be an isolated example. London Country would prove to be largely immune from such a situation, but the Government's longer term intentions were clear; all bus services would become completely de-regulated with potentially serious implications for the continuance of rural routes.

As 1982 began, the levels of service run by London Country required further reductions to save more costs and reduce levels of public subsidy. Kent County Council – although generally supportive – were finding their level of subsidies too great a burden and announced that they needed to save £100,000 per annum, leading to yet another round of revisions and service cuts to routes run from Dartford and Northfleet. Although the combined numbers of buses rostered between the two garages went down by only three, evening and Sunday mileage was reduced again to the extent that the total Sunday run out dropped to just 11 buses compared to the 20 required a decade earlier. The general level of Kent's subsidies (and for that matter Berkshire as well) was also lower than Surrey and

When the first BLs arrived in 1973 it was intended that some would be allocated to Northfleet, but it was found that their extra width was a problem on the narrow lane in Southfleet on the 490 and between Betsham and High Cross on the 450. It was not until September 1974 when the narrower BNs arrived that Northfleet received some for the 450, 489, and 490. The 450 timetable between Gravesend and Dartford through the lanes was minimal, but an hourly service ran between Dartford and Bean. BN 25 has arrived at Bean and is running round the terminal loop before returning to Dartford. Northfleet had to retain one BN into 1980 for the shopping service along the single track lane between Westwood and Betsham. (John Miller)

Hertfordshire who had always taken a more pragmatic and supportive position, so that London Country's fare scales in Kent and Berkshire were of necessity higher. This did not encourage as many passengers as it might have done, a factor which reduced London Country's potential revenue, in turn putting more pressure on subsidies.

In Essex, after the 339 had been cut back from Brentwood to Ongar, leaving that section to Eastern National, the leg from Epping, largely through open countryside, was often run non-stop apart from a handful of local passengers between Epping and North Weald. In December, London Country cut the route back to Epping, with London Transport running a new 201 route from Loughton through Epping to Ongar instead, subsidised by Essex County Council.

Like Kent, Surrey was equally concerned about levels of subsidies. In the previous six years, London Country's fares in Surrey had increased more than two and a half times – significantly more than the general level of inflation which itself had been extremely high. Steep increases in fares – though essential – had driven away passengers, total numbers going down by almost a quarter in the same period, and although London Country's overall revenue had increased, it had been more than offset by increased costs. Surrey's revenue support to London Country had therefore had to increase steeply to keep pace, and despite substantial service cuts, had increased by more than 60% in the same six-year period. But London Country were not the only operator Surrey had to deal with, as the subsidies being paid to London Transport were proportionately much higher, in particular those on their suburban routes which ran out into the north of the county. London Country's operating costs per mile were almost 30% less than those of London Transport, who still clung to outdated operating practices and higher fixed costs in premises and overheads. In April 1982, after lengthy planning and negotiations, London Transport's 280 and 280A to Lower Kingswood and Walton-on-the-Hill were withdrawn, and together with other revisions, London Country took over parts of routes south of Sutton and Banstead. The overall effect was that Surrey were able to save around £150,000 per annum, a considerable sum, but to the further detriment of London Transport.

The first AEC Reliance coaches, which had started the turnaround in Green

Line's fortunes in 1977, had come to the end of their five year lease and from April began to be returned to the dealer. The terms of the lease required London Country to refurbish the coaches before returning them, and this gave rise to some difficulties. 42 new Leyland Tigers had been ordered to replace the first batch of 30 Reliances together with the 12 high capacity RNs purchased second hand from Barton, and represented the next development in the continuing turn-around of Green Line. However, delivery of the Tigers which had first been anticipated in February was delayed until June due to a strike at the Leyland chassis plant, and by some modifications which Eastern Coaches Works had to make to strengthen certain sections of the bodywork. The late delivery which then continued over nearly six months necessitated many reallocations to cover for those earlier RSs and RBs which had to be refurbished. Nonetheless, all the new coaches, designated TL, were in service by the year end.

British Leyland had ended production of the Bristol VR in 1981, replacing it with the Leyland Olympian. Prior to the Olympian, they had produced the Titan which in many ways had been conceived as a double-deck version of the National in that it was completely standardised with a full height body, offering little variation to suit the requirements of different operators. Whilst London Transport took large numbers of Titans it had little success otherwise, and was replaced by the Olympian which was a much more conventional design offering full or low height bodywork. London Country had ordered a first batch of 30, all of which were in service by July, allowing more progress in allocating double deckers to routes where the capacity of single deckers was still a problem on some journeys. The Olympian proved very successful, almost 3000 being produced in its first six years, London Country taking in 75 buses and 15 long-chassis coach versions.

On 21st November, the new garage at Crawley, which had been built next to the Tinsley Green central works, opened to replace the old garage on the Brighton road near Crawley town centre. The 'C Line' town service network introduced in 1978 to replace the haphazard route patterns which had grown over the previous twenty years as Crawley expanded, had proved to be far more cost effective and profitable. In addition, the expansion of Gatwick Airport had seen large scale commercial development of the whole area between there and Crawley. These factors had increased Crawley's workload to the extent that the allocation had actually increased slightly over the previous decade despite so many cuts elsewhere. The old garage occupied a valuable site on the London Road near the town centre which could be sold for redevelopment, and the new garage was a welcome improvement to Crawley's operations.

In west Surrey, the 'Weyfarer' MAP scheme had given Tillingbourne a greater foothold along the Guildford to Cranleigh corridor, adding to their operations in the rural area bounded by Guildford, Horsham and Dorking, but they still did not operate the main links between these three towns. London Country's 425 between Dorking and Guildford had become one of Surrey's most expensive routes in terms of subsidy, and Tillingbourne saw an opportunity to reduce Surrey's subsidy by taking over the route. In September 1982 therefore, they made further proposals to take over not only the 425, but also the 412 while other independents would take over the 439 and 449. Once again these came to nothing at the time, but Tillingbourne were not to be deterred in their ambitions, and 12 months later they put forward even more radical proposals. These posed a serious threat to London Country, and would have led to the closure of Dorking garage, so in an effort to consolidate their increasingly fragile position along the Dorking to

Guildford corridor, they took the radical step of introducing another innovative Green Line route. Numbered 762, operated jointly with Southdown and Alder Valley, it ran from Brighton to Reading via Crawley, Dorking, and Guildford, with an end-to-end running time of just over three and a half hours on a route more than 90 miles long. The already successful 773 which ran hourly between Brighton and Gatwick was retained, so that the new 762 increased the service between Crawley and Brighton. Running to a two-hourly headway, the 762 stopped only at Merrow, Gomshall and Westcott between Dorking and Guildford, but sought to encourage additional longer distance passengers between main centres, particularly Dorking, Reigate and Guildford where the 'stopping' bus services were in rapid decline. London Country's contribution to the 762 was two coaches added to Dorking's allocation. It was originally intended to start the route in September 1982, but British Rail objected since it posed direct competition to the Redhill–Guildford–Reading train service. The Traffic Commissioners took the view however that the 762 *'was in the public interest'* and overruled the objection, so that the route began on 23rd January 1983. At the same time the 762 was introduced Tillingbourne at last made some headway in the area when they took over McCann's routes from Forest Green. The Friday only route via Coldharbour into Dorking was withdrawn, but on the long-standing Guildford – Forest Green – Horsham route they added some extra journeys between Guildford and Gomshall in between London Country's 425 service. The 425 continued its hourly headway seven days a week, but little was left of Dorking's other rural mileage. After the withdrawal of the 412 extension to Cranleigh, the timetable to Holmbury St Mary and Sutton was down to just five journeys, with only four to Newdigate on the 439 and two to Ranmore on Tuesday and Friday mornings only. Dorking still ran the hourly 714 Green Line between Horsham and Kingston with six journeys on into central London, and put out two buses on the 414 to Croydon. The busy road from Dorking to Leatherhead which had once enjoyed four coaches and three buses an

The 773 began in April 1981 as a return facility on Saturdays from Westcott and Dorking to Brighton, an additional return on Tuesdays being added in August. In May 1982, the route was diverted via Horley and renumbered 776, the 773 number then being used for a new route from Gatwick Airport via Crawley and Hassocks to Brighton with some journeys continuing to Hove. Operated jointly by London Country and Southdown, the 773 was branded 'Sealine' and was a further addition to the turnaround of the Green Line network. Displaying the 'Sealine' branding, RS 148 picks up near Churchill Square in Brighton (Barry Le Jeune)

hour, and where huge queues of passengers had once waited at the foot of Boxhill for Green Lines home, now had just one coach per hour. In the heyday of Dorking's Green Line routes, its run out had required 16 coaches and 64 crew seven days a week, even without reliefs and duplicates, but now this was down to six coaches and 15 drivers. Their drastically reduced bus routes were all that remained of London Transport's once frequent Surrey Hills services. A radical and bold review of Dorking's operations could have closed the garage in the late 1960s and transferred its operations among Reigate, Leatherhead and Guildford, but such a move would of course have been unthinkable within London Transport's rigid approach. Fifteen years later however, with the continuous culling of its services, Dorking's position had by 1982 become extremely precarious.

January 1983 also saw further fundamental changes to routes in the north of Surrey around the Kingston, Weybridge and Staines area. Once again London Transport were the principal losers as Surrey sought to reduce its support for bus services in the area, many of which were little changed from the post-war network. London Transport's routes 116 and 203 to Staines were reduced in frequency, and much of the Kingston to Walton service was withdrawn in favour of London Country's new 456, which ran from Chertsey and St Peter's Hospital via Walton to Kingston. A major change was the complete withdrawal of the 219 from Kingston to Weybridge which was replaced by London Country's new 437 from Guildford over the former 463 route to Weybridge and on to Kingston over the withdrawn 219. Over the section from Hersham to Kingston, it was timed to run to a joint timetable with the 218 (Kingston – Staines) which London Transport retained. The former 264 (Kingston – Sunbury – Hersham) which had only run to a limited 40-minute headway had always been a 'secondary' route, and had been abandoned by London Transport five years earlier, since Surrey could no longer support it. London Country also introduced some new links to Heathrow by extending the Guildford to Staines route, and there were many other minor changes. Once again, Surrey achieved savings, London Country's allocations at Addlestone and Guildford benefited from more work, but London Transport's work from Kingston suffered a substantial reduction.

The NBC annual report for 1982 showed a reduction in mileage run of 8% over the previous three years, but an 18% reduction in staffing numbers and vehicles over the same period. This had produced an improved use of resources, and the report commented that the NBC and its subsidiaries were at last coming to terms with the enormous retrenchment which had taken place during the previous decade. The operating surplus had almost completely been negated by huge interest costs on capital loans, but at least a surplus could be reported. The report commented however *that improved performance cannot mask the underlying deep concern that public transport deserves better support – both financial and from Government in terms of better co-ordinated systems'.* This was a direct challenge to the Thatcher government which came under frequent criticism at the time for its perceived lack of transport policies and sufficient financial support.

In 1981, politics played an extremely influential role in the future strategy for London's buses. The GLC came under Labour control in May, and five months later introduced the 'Fares Fair' policy, which had formed an important part of their campaign in which they had committed to lowering bus, train, and Underground fares within the GLC area. Its main objective was to cut fares by 25% in an attempt to encourage additional passengers and cut congestion. Central Government quickly stated that there would be no additional state funding to

subsidise this, but the GLC went ahead and introduced the policy on the basis that any revenue shortfall would be met by levying a supplementary rate from the London Boroughs. The lengthy battles which followed to test the legality of the policy, ending up as they did in the High Court, need not be part of this book, but what did emerge was a recognition of the need for a fundamental review of the way in which London Transport was funded. In February 1981, the House of Commons Select Transport Committee set up an inquiry to look at these issues, and late in 1983, a White Paper was published proposing fundamental changes not only to funding, but to the way in which London's bus route network would be organised. A new body – London Regional Transport (LRT) – was to be given the principal remit of reducing costs and the burden on taxpayers, bus services being opened to competition as was already the case outside London. Operators – not just London Transport – could apply to LRT to run any commercial service, and LRT could seek tenders for other routes which required subsidy. Although the GLC had been much criticised for its 'Fares Fair' policy, and the instability which followed the High Court decision that the policy was not legal and should be reversed, it had highlighted the ever increasing levels of public subsidy for London's bus services. This subsidy had risen from £6.5 million in 1970 to a staggering £370 million by 1983. This was a 13-fold increase even after accounting for the levels of high inflation in the 1970s, during which time London Transport had doubled fares anyway. The creation of LRT, and competition for bus routes in London, would have a profound effect on London Transport as it then was, and would at last force changes to the inflexible operating methods which were so entrenched and little changed from the 1930s. Operators on the periphery of London, London Country and Eastern National in particular, would benefit from several new routes over the following few years as LRT's tendering process gained momentum.

In April 1979, the 704 was reduced to run only between London and Windsor, the service from Tunbridge Wells being renumbered 706. An hourly headway was maintained as far as Bromley, but reduced to two hourly into London for most of the day. The text refers to the drastic cuts to bus routes in April 1981 which included the withdrawal of the 454 via Weald Village, the 706 being diverted from the main road as replacement. Most journeys were also diverted via Halstead to replace the reduced bus service. TP 65 was one of the batch of Plaxton bodied Leyland Tigers delivered in 1984 and is in the later attractive green and cream livery.
(Barry Le Jeune)

The 741 was a second route operated jointly with Alder Valley from Whitehill and Hindhead to London, and began on the same day as the 740 to Farnham. RP 25 was London Country's last one, and Guildford turned it out on 18th February 1984 to work an afternoon journey as far as Godalming on its last day in service. It has a good load on board as it pulls out of Butterwick in Hammersmith (Mike Harris)

By late 1983, London Country had withdrawn almost all of the hapless RP coaches. The last ones at Harlow had been withdrawn in the year, leaving a handful at Guildford and Addlestone with one at Leatherhead used for contract work. Very few of them had managed ten years in service, and their departure signified almost the end of the poorly manufactured products of the early 1970s which had beset London Country with so many problems. When they arrived in early 1972, they were intended to be the forefront of a new generation of Green Line coaches, and in their original livery with large 'Green Line' fleetnames, they combined the long standing traditions with an updated image. The crisis caused by a lack of spares in the mid-1970s and their general unreliability effectively ended the majority of their Green Line careers after less than five years in service. Whilst a number continued to run a few Green Line routes, the others which remained were demoted to bus work, and this dwindled steadily after 1980. By September 1983, only four remained in service; two each at Addlestone and Guildford, both of which had operated RPs from their introduction, initially on the 715, 716 and 716A routes and later on the Guildford – Addlestone – Staines/ Walton bus routes. My own last journey on an RP had been a year earlier on RP 2 late on a Saturday afternoon on a 384 from Hertford to Stevenage. Only ten years old, it looked shabby and in poor condition, but was better suited to the gentle rural run through the Hertfordshire lanes with me as the only passenger most of the way. The last four RPs were taken out of service without ceremony, Addlestone's last one running its final day in service in February 1984.

London Country and United Counties exchanged their operations on the 314 and 383 in November 1977. By then the 314 timetable had been reduced to only four return journeys, all that was left of the once hourly Rushden to London service run by Birch since the 1930s. Stevenage ran the bus light to Welwyn to take up service, and on Saturdays, ran additional journeys from Hitchin to Stevenage on the 303 between the 314 timetable plus one afternoon 303C works journey to and from Hitchin during the week. Stevenage was one of the last northern area garages to retain RPs, and on 12th April 1980, RP 15 stops to set down in Codicote (Mike Harris)

Following the withdrawal of the Bristol BLs in 1980/81, many BNs were withdrawn in 1983. Northfleet's last two were withdrawn in January when the lane through Betsham was approved for SNBs, and SNBs displaced by double deckers on busier routes ousted four more from St Albans in April. By the year end, their numbers had been reduced to just five which had to be retained at Amersham for journeys on the 349 and 394 which terminated at Chesham Moor, a housing estate a mile or so from the town centre where the turning point required a tight reverse which was not approved for anything larger. Although their ride quality was poor, the BLs and BNs had at least served the purpose for which they were intended, but continuous service reductions had rendered them surplus well before the end of a normal service life. Because of the restriction at Chesham Moor however, Amersham's BNs outlasted the others by some time, and in October 1984 what proved to be my last journey on a BN was a run from Chesham to Great Missenden on BN 57. This was a Saturday lunchtime journey from Chesham, and the bus departed three quarters full. Most though proved to be short distance passengers, and by the time the bus left Chartridge, there were fewer than half a dozen left on board. When two more got off at Lee Common, an elderly lady and I were the only remaining passengers. She alighted in Ballinger to be replaced by another elderly lady, but nobody else was picked up, and we ran at 'regulation speed', still arriving at Great Missenden a few minutes early. Fifteen years earlier, there were eight journeys from Chesham to Missenden on Saturdays, with four more as far as Lee Common, and in 1967 I had travelled the

same route on RF 304 with a full load from Chesham, arriving in Missenden still with half a load, passengers having been dropped off and picked up all along the route. By the time of this last BN journey, there were just four journeys to Missenden and only two in the opposite direction, timed only for morning or afternoon shopping in Chesham, and without heavy subsidy would not have run at all. By then, the Missenden route had become a circular, running back to Amersham along the main road. After United Counties had withdrawn from their share of the 359 in 1964, London Transport continued with a two-hourly service through Missenden, but over the next 15 years, it had been cut back and back, and by 1984 just a couple of journeys on Thursday and Saturday were all that was left of the service through Little Missenden into Amersham.

When Windsor garage had first opened in March 1933, it was an important base, and in the 1950s had a scheduled run out of almost 100, increased further by the many Green Line duplicates at weekends when any spare bus would be borrowed from other Country or Central area garages. Windsor was a major tourist destination, and the Green Line allocation had been the largest of all Country area garages with the exception of Romford's run out for the 721. Before the war, Slough was a relatively small town on the Great West Road, but the expansion of the estates at Britwell and Wexham Court Farm in the 1950s saw significant growth around the Town. More housing to the east towards Langley and Colnbrook, and the expansion of Heathrow Airport, accelerated Slough's expansion and importance, so that by the 1970s it was a much more important transport centre than Windsor. In the 20 years to the mid-1970s Windsor garage's total run out had almost halved, the great majority of visitors came by car, and much of its bus route operations involved costly dead mileage to and from Slough, together with the unproductive costs of ferrying crews back and forth. Indeed, on Sundays in 1975, three RMLs were rostered solely as crew ferry buses to and from Slough – a necessary operational cost, but equally a financial burden.

For many years there had been no Sunday buses to places such as Leith Hill, Peaslake and Holmbury St Mary. The area however was very popular at weekends, and so in 1977 Surrey County Council looked at how a service might be run just with one bus, aimed specifically at encouraging walkers. The result was the 417 Ramblers Bus which began on 5th June that year and ran four journeys in a long circular route centred on Dorking. It proved very successful, almost covering its costs in the first season so that in 1978 it ran for a longer period, carrying three times the number of passengers and returning a profit. London Country frequently used their 'showbus' RF 202 on the route to encourage greater use, and on 17th August 1980, it is approaching Burrows Cross from Peaslake before turning down the single track lane to Gomshall. On busy days, duplication was often necessary, and in this view an SNB runs behind as the duplicate bus. (Mike Harris)

The long wheelbase Olympian coaches mentioned in the text were very impressive and were put to good use on the 720 from Gravesend to London replacing RBs to provide more capacity.. They were also used at weekends on London Country's National Express contract for the London to Poole service which required duplication and high capacity to carry the large numbers of passengers. LRC 5 displays the distinctive livery used on these coaches which were a further improvement in the turnaround of the Green Line brand. (Ian Pringle)

The 'Thamesline' MAP scheme in May 1980 had reduced Windsor's run-out still further and concentrated a greater proportion of its operations around Slough, leaving Windsor as an expensive overhead and inefficient operating base. On 29th July 1984 therefore, Windsor garage was closed, to be replaced by a new garage in Slough with a scheduled run out of 25 buses and 14 coaches, a total which would subsequently increase with some National Express work. Except for one double decker for contract work, the buses were all Leyland Nationals, concentrated mainly on town services, although the half hourly 443 and 458 routes to Uxbridge via Iver Heath or Langley still ran together with the 441 High Wycombe route. These 25 buses compared with a run-out of 65 for summer 1955, and even at the end of London Transport's days it was still 42. More service revisions also brought about new route numbers, doing away with the last of the traditional 400 series numbers on Slough Town services with new routes numbered in the sequence 90 to 96.

In March 1984 a batch of new double deck Leyland Olympian coaches was delivered and went to Northfleet for the 720 route which, after its inception as a commuter route in November 1981, had grown into an all-day route with increasing numbers of passengers. It bore no resemblance to the former 701/702 routes to London, its success being that it ran non-stop from the outskirts of Gravesend to the City serving several useful points before terminating at Victoria. These new coaches were a significant improvement to the route's image, and London Country was also able to use them on other work. There was no Sunday service on the 720, and the Saturday service required fewer coaches, so the spares were used on the London to Poole National Express service on which London Country were contracted to run some journeys. This was an extremely busy coach service, often requiring duplication at weekends, and the new Olympians were ideal.

A month after this, two more innovative Green Line routes were started. The 765 from Stevenage and Hertford to Brighton ran four times a day, and the 795 from Southend to Brighton five times a day. In a little over seven years since the process had begun with the introduction of the 707 and 717 in January 1977, the entire post-war network of Green Line routes had been abandoned to be replaced by routes that actually attracted passengers. The outer 'country' sections of many of the original routes were still covered, and the 724, 725, and 727 introduced by London Transport continued to be successful, but the overall network was unrecognisable from the loss-making unattractive service left by London Transport in 1970. The 723 was in fact the only remaining original route, although the Grays to Tilbury section had been abandoned, and it had been extended from Aldgate, through the City to Victoria in August 1981. After the halcyon days of the east London routes had passed, the terminus at Aldgate was unattractive to passengers who wanted to travel further into central London, and the extension to Victoria was an obvious improvement that more imaginative management by London Transport could have made years earlier. By summer 1984 the expansion of Green Line routes required 194 coaches running profitable routes, compared to the schedules at the end of 1976 which required 141 coaches almost all running loss-making routes. In addition to these 194 coaches, Harlow garage had 11 buses rostered to the bus routes which covered the old 720 road from Bishops Stortford and the previous section of the 724 from Harlow to Romford. Godstone also had four allocated to the 419 express Croydon to East Grinstead route which had partly replaced the old 719. Another seven coaches were allocated permanently to National Express routes, split between Guildford, Staines and Slough. Guildford and Staines shared workings from Heathrow to Manchester which also involved the coaches running two return trips daily between Manchester and Leeds, while Slough worked from Gatwick to Bradford and the 12-hour long haul from Reading to Aberdeen. A more prosaic curiosity was the joint operation of the new 765 between Crawley and Hertford garages which involved swapping a coach each day, the Crawley coach working two evening journeys on the 350/351 from Hertford to Bishops Stortford to make full use of it. Why Hertford didn't use a National, which ran the rest of the timetable, is unknown.

The text refers to Guildford's allocation to the National Express service from Heathrow to Manchester and Leeds, and a few Green Line coaches were repainted into National Express livery. London Country took delivery of 42 Leyland TRCL TRC/TL11 Tigers in 1982/83 and they proved to be extremely successful with plenty of power, smooth gearchange and a high level of passenger comfort. The first batch had ECW bodies, the second batch these attractive Duple bodies as shown here on TD 33 which was new in 1983. When not on National Express work they were used for Green Line service and it has pulled up at the 715 stop in Commercial Road outside Guildford's recently completed bus station. (Colin Brown)

The non-stop commuter routes from London to Hemel Hempstead via the M1 proved very successful, the 758 beginning in September 1981, and the 759 in October 1982. The 758 operated four journeys each day, while the 759 provided one peak hour journey to the Long Chaulden and Gadebridge areas. In July 1983, TD 19 is at the top of Park Lane on the evening return 759 journey. It was one the 42 Leyland Tigers ordered in 1982 and is in the updated Green Line livery employed on the second generation of coaches. (Mike Harris)

This expansion of Green Line routes had benefited several garages. Northfleet which had six coaches for the 725 in 1976 now required 17, 14 of which were for the 720 and the London–Poole National Express service mentioned above. St Albans had run six SNCs on the loss-making 712 and 713 in late 1976, but now ran 18 coaches including ten for the non-stop 757 Luton Airport to London route. Hemel Hempstead had increased their allocation from five in 1976 to 15 in 1984, nine of which ran the non-stop commuter and shopping services into central London. In 1977, Amersham had no Green Line work at all after its last two duties went with the withdrawal of the 710 five years earlier. By 1984 it required 11 coaches for the London to Thame/Oxford routes and the 788 commuter and shopping service. In addition to their National Express work, Guildford and Staines had both doubled their allocations. None of the coach fleet was more than five years old and since the start of the 707/717, with the new RS Reliances, more than 300 new coaches had come into the fleet by the beginning of 1984. Although this represented a large investment, it had proved very worthwhile and more than justified the bold decision taken in 1976 to completely revise Green Line operations.

Tillingbourne's continuing ambitions to gain more of a foothold in Surrey came to the fore once again during the summer of 1984. The previous year, in concert with Safeguard and Blue Saloon, the other Guildford independents, they had proposed a plan for service alterations which they calculated would provide Surrey with large savings in subsidies. Tillingbourne had wanted Surrey's support for their applications for services along the Guildford to Dorking and Guildford to Cranleigh corridors, together with Guildford town services to Merrow and Burpham, all of which had been resisted by both Alder Valley and London Country for obvious reasons. In the wake of Alder Valley's painful restructuring, the routes to Cranleigh were among their more profitable from Guildford, and

SM 488 shows the awful overall NBC leaf green livery as it stands at one of the temporary stops used while Guildford bus station was being redeveloped in 1980. The newer blinds with the cramped route numbers were a backward step from the old Johnston script. The 408A was one of the Guildford town services which Tillingbourne would have taken over if the proposals referred to in the text had been adopted. (Mike Harris)

London Country's Guildford garage relied on town services for a good proportion of its revenue. Tillingbourne criticised both London Country and Alder Valley for not having rationalised their Guildford operations more radically, despite the changes brought about by the 1980 'Weyfarer' MAP scheme. They suggested that their proposals for taking over the Town services they did not already run would allow London Country and Alder Valley to rationalise their operations to the extent that one of the depots could be closed and services run by just one operator. This would remove a large element of fixed cost, and lead to less subsidy being required for the routes from Guildford which would remain with either of the NBC companies. In the financial year 1982/1983, Surrey had paid no less than £501,000 in subsidies – the bulk of it to London Country and Alder Valley – for Guildford, Dorking and Horsham area routes. Of the independent operators, only Tillingbourne received the nominal sum of £35,000 for its rural routes, and the potential savings from these radical proposals were therefore significant. Any reductions in subsidy would result in Tillingbourne and the other operators taking on some of the NBC routes in any event, since it was supposed that neither London Country or Alder Valley would be prepared to continue to operate routes without the current levels of subsidy. The two NBC companies were, not surprisingly, alarmed by Tillingbourne's proposals, and submitted their own counter proposals to take over most of Safeguard and Tillingbourne's operations, claiming that the additional revenue would enable cost savings and reduce subsidy levels through economy of scale.

Up to this point, Surrey had been reluctant to disturb the status quo, but this time however, in January 1984, they commissioned an independent report to assess the differing proposals of Tillingbourne and the other operators. Perhaps unsurprisingly, the report, completed in October 1984, recommended acceptance of Tillingbourne's proposals as soon as possible since substantial savings would indeed accrue. Tillingbourne would take over the 425, and what little was left of the 412 to Holmbury St Mary and Sutton, proposing a 'village minibus' which would also take on the Friday morning journeys to Ranmore. The need for a through link from Dorking to Guildford would largely be satisfied by the two hourly 762 Green Line route, but this had few stops, and there remained a need for a service from Gomshall and Shere via Albury and Chilworth into Guildford. Alder Valley's routes to Cranleigh and on to Horsham proved a main sticking point however, Tillingbourne initially not being prepared to run the corridor to Dorking without that to Cranleigh as well. The negotiations which followed were complex, time consuming and at times acrimonious, particularly with Alder Valley who stood to lose the most in terms of both mileage run and subsidy. After six months of negotiations, agreement was finally reached and the new network came into operation on 14th April 1985. Alder Valley wished to withdraw from the 762 route, so London Country recast it as 773 between Guildford and Brighton, jointly operated with Southdown. It ran to an hourly headway during the week, with no late evening service after around 7.00pm except Saturdays when there was one late journey into Guildford and back. The Sunday 773 timetable was cut back to only five journeys, which was light years away from the 15-minute afternoon headway of summer 1955 on the 425, and required just a single coach from Dorking. The 425 which had run unchanged for over 50 years was finally withdrawn, with Tillingbourne running from Guildford via Chilworth to Shere and Gomshall on an hourly headway on routes 25 and 44 which ran on through Peaslake to Cranleigh, or to Forest Green over the old McCann route. The 412 was covered by Tillingbourne's 'Village Minibus' service 22 which ran four journeys a day Monday to Friday and three Saturday between Shere and Dorking via Sutton and Holmbury St Mary, the same minibus being used to run the single Friday morning shopping journey from Ranmore into Dorking and back. West of Dorking, other than the 773 Green Line, all that London Country had left was a Monday to Friday early morning journey from Shere via Holmbury St Mary into Dorking, still numbered 412, plus a morning schoolday only 412 from Sutton and Holmbury into Dorking, and back in the afternoon. They also retained five journeys just to Westcott (six on schooldays) run mainly for a commuter link to Dorking Station. On Saturday, only one Westcott journey remained at 11.14pm from Dorking Station, run off route 449, the bus running back empty to the garage. The 414 to Croydon was withdrawn in the evening so that the last departure from Dorking was just after 6.30pm during the week, and just after 7.00pm Saturdays, whilst the Sunday service consisted of just six journeys on a two hourly headway run entirely by Reigate.

The Tillingbourne minibus which worked the 22 was timed to connect at Shere with the service to and from Guildford, but with only three or four journeys a day the link from Albury and Chilworth into Dorking, which had run at least hourly for the previous 15 years (and more frequently still before that) was reduced to being of little use. The three Saturday journeys did operate through from Shere into Guildford, but offered scant replacement. Initially there were complaints at the loss of the facility, but the truth was that by 1984 – and even for some years before – the numbers of passengers who used the service was too small to justify its continuation, a far cry from the six or seven RFs once needed to meet the demand. There were also occasions when the capacity of the 16 seat minibus proved inadequate, but the service generally met what minimal demand remained.

The changes led to understandable discontent from Dorking Garage's staff, even to the extent of trying to prevent Tillingbourne using Dorking Bus Station on the Village Minibus 22 route. Dorking was left with a Monday to Friday run-out of just seven buses, plus two more on Schooldays and one for contract work. Four of these were rostered to the 414, which was Dorking's main operation, while the remainder ran the odd 412 journeys noted above, four journeys to Newdigate, two to Boxhill, and the hourly 449 town service. All but two were back in the garage by just after 7.00pm. The Saturday run-out was only six, and none at all on Sundays except one bus used to run the three circular journeys round the 417 summer only 'Ramblers Bus' from the end of May until the beginning of September. Eight coaches were still rostered Monday to Saturday, but only five on Sundays.

SM 530 is mentioned in chapter one. It was the bus I travelled on from Tonbridge on a 454 in 1972 and which had to be taken out of service at Sevenoaks having overheated with smoke coming up through the rear seats over the engine compartment – a common fault with many of them. It later spent 15 months at Dunton Green out of use with a long term defect before being returned to service in April 1975. At the end of 1976 it was loaned to Windsor for a month and then transferred to Amersham where it was withdrawn in October 1979 having been in actual use for a little under six years. Here it is leaving Orpington with a National behind on the 493 town service. (Mike Harris)

Twenty years earlier, when Surrey Hills routes were still buoyant despite falling traffic, Dorking had run out 18 buses and 14 coaches Monday to Friday, and on Sundays 4 RT, 6 RF and 14 RF coaches which, between them all, required around 40 drivers and 32 conductors for the day's work. Now Sundays required just 10 drivers plus an extra one for the 417 during the short summer period. All this left Dorking garage in a position where its continued operation could no longer be commercially justified. Operation of the 414, 714, and 773 could have been transferred to Reigate, Leatherhead and Guildford respectively, and even the one bus for the 449 could have been run out of Leatherhead. The minimal service on the 412, 439 and 451 (Boxhill service) would almost certainly have been attractive to Tillingbourne, but even if London Country withdrew, Surrey would have been no worse off in subsidising another operator. There was no justification for retaining Dorking, but it was allocated additional work when London Country won the LRT tender to take over the 293 from Epsom to Wimbledon from London Transport. This involved much dead mileage between Epsom and Dorking which seemed absurd when Leatherhead was much closer, but Dorking required six double deckers to run the 293, and a further bus was added to work an additional contract duty. Nevertheless this did not alter the fact that Dorking was no longer viable. Whether or not the additional allocation for the 293 was to stave off inevitable closure is not known, but in the end it would be another five years before the garage finally closed.

Dorking was not the only garage to suffer severe reductions in the April 1985 changes, some of Reigate's town services being heavily cut back. The timetable between Reigate and Redhill through Meadvale was reduced to hourly with no evening service. A decade earlier, it had been half hourly, running all day until 11.00pm at night. The former 447 route via Batts Hill was reduced to just five daytime shopping journeys compared to hourly into late evening a decade before. Even the large estate at Merstham which had always provided large numbers of regular passengers had the service reduced, the daytime Saturday timetable being cut back from five to three journeys an hour, and no service on Sunday morning until 10.30am. The rural 440 to Caterham – hourly a decade before – was reduced to two shopping journeys on Tuesday and Friday only.

In the previous few years, the pace of change had continued to accelerate. The last conductors had gone, Green Line had been restored to profitability, and the MAP schemes plus many other service revisions had reduced costs. London Country's fortunes had largely been restored. The Transport Act had been the subject of some criticism, but had generally proved successful in sweeping away much bureaucracy and giving operators more flexibility, particularly for express services from which London Country had gained many benefits. The success of the Transport Act however provided the Government with the impetus for what would prove to be the greatest changes of all. In a few short years, the large territorial companies which had operated since pre-war days with little change and minimal competition would cease to exist.

4 Break-up and Privatisation

In July 1984, the Government published a White Paper, simply titled 'Buses' which proposed a fundamental change in the way bus services – particularly rural ones – would be run. It set out, as had been widely anticipated following the 1980 Act, proposals for the complete deregulation of all bus services, allowing a market open to free competition The Traffic Commissioners and licensing regulations would be abolished. The White Paper also recognised that many of the NBC companies in their present state could not be what the proposals described as 'low cost competitive units', It would therefore be necessary to split them into smaller companies in preparation for them to be sold off to the private sector.

The White Paper also took account of the fact that in a competitive market, almost all rural bus services, and many other essential routes, could never be commercially viable. Money would therefore be made available – initially a sum of £20 million over four years – to maintain rural routes during the transition to a point where it was anticipated that operation of essential routes would become established with new operators and affordable levels of subsidy where necessary.

Deregulation would create a demand for buses which could be used on a variety of routes. In 1988, Dennis produced the Dart which was built in three different lengths, and was so successful that more than 11000 were built over an 18 year period. London Country North West purchased some for routes won in tendering. In 1992, DC 7 in 'Watford Wide' livery is working a 258 to Harrow – one of a number of former suburban routes lost by London Transport to London Country under the TfL tendering programme and which are also green no more. (Capital Transport)

Money was also to be made available in the form of grants to encourage innovation in providing rural services, such as the use of minibuses and community based local schemes. In addition to the division of the larger operators – who were almost all NBC subsidiaries – there were to be provisions to prevent restrictive practices between operators which might limit competition. The size of many of the NBC companies, their fixed cost bases, and the levels of subsidy on which they had to rely, made them unattractive to private ownership, and so the break-up of these and of the NBC as a whole was fundamental to achieving competition and reducing public subsidy. Predictably, the proposals met with much criticism, those opposing the reforms arguing that wholesale deregulation and competition would mean the end of rural bus services, with many other former important links being reduced to a skeleton timetable consisting of a few profitable journeys. Critics argued that the 'Yeowarts Fiasco' referred to earlier would be widely repeated – although it proved to be largely isolated. In its 1984 report, the Chairman of NBC criticised the proposals on the basis that they would undermine all that NBC had achieved during previous years in terms of reducing costs, and initiatives such as MAP schemes. The NBC had done much in their efforts to win back passengers, had become profitable, and were in a position to continue paying interest and large sums from its capital debt. The White Paper's proposals would, it argued, fragment the industry and create great uncertainty.

London Country perhaps illustrated the issues that faced many operators. In its 15th year since formation, it had displayed great initiative in winning back passengers with wholesale changes to the Green Line brand, it had been through three major MAP reorganisations, and overcome what had seemed at times insurmountable problems to become profitable. The bus route network was barely recognisable from that which it inherited. Four peripheral garages (Tring, Luton, High Wycombe and East Grinstead) had been shut, Windsor and Crawley had been replaced, and a new Central Works built. The fleet had been reduced substantially, the maximum run-out of 906 required for bus services in January 1970 having been drastically reduced by almost 30%, with more than a third of these operating profitable town services or routes in urban conurbations such as Gravesend, Dartford and around Grays. Yet, despite all this, it was one of the NBC's biggest subsidiaries and required a substantial fixed overhead to maintain its network. A quirk of history meant that because it surrounded London with no 'centre' to its area, it was more difficult to manage, and its passenger base came from some of the most affluent areas of the country with higher levels of both car ownership and traffic congestion. Despite the complete turnaround from the shambles it inherited, London Country as it was could not be a low cost operator in a free competitive market. Other operators such as Eastern Counties, United, Lincolnshire, Ribble and Crosville were simply too large in terms of their geographic operating areas, large parts of which were sparsely populated, and could never be profitable without an enormous level of subsidy which in turn was too great a burden on the taxpayer. Others like Western/Southern National, Devon General, Hants & Dorset and Southdown, although benefiting more than most from an influx of summer holidaymakers, and with some profitable centres, were also too large geographically, and needed to be sub-divided in order to reduce their fixed cost base.

Following the White Paper, The Transport Bill published in January 1985 set the deadline for the abolition of licensing and the start of the competitive market on 1st October 1986. There is no need to detail all the effects of the Act since

London Country's rural routes into Orpington were all replaced on 16th August 1986 by the 'Roundabout' network which was one of the low cost stand-alone operations set up by London Transport to win tendered routes. Two days before London Country ceased operations, SNB 254 comes down the narrow lane at Well Hill on the 1.44pm 431 Sevenoaks to Orpington on a route which was operated with RTs until the end of 1966. (Author)

these have been well documented elsewhere, but the underlying effect of the legislation meant the end both of bus operation and large territorial companies as they had existed for more than half a century. It was the seismic change which would alter the industry completely.

In October 1985, the section of the M25 between Wisley and Reigate opened, and allowed the start of a faster non-stop Heathrow to Gatwick service which London Country marketed as 'Speedlink'. New Berkhof bodied Leyland Tigers were used to run a frequent 20-minute headway requiring 14 coaches, seven each from Staines and Crawley. With traffic levels on the M25 then at a fraction of what they would become, the original journey time was only 50 minutes and the drivers had 'cellphones' (then a very new innovation) to warn each other of delays en-route. The original 747 route had been an outstanding success having carried more than 300,000 passengers in the previous year, so on the same day that the new 'Speedlink' service began, the 747 was extended north from Heathrow to Hemel Hempstead, Luton and Stevenage, giving many new links to main line rail routes, and replacing the former two hourly 750 route.

Following its formation LRT had begun putting routes out to tender, and in July 1985 London Country won the contract for the 313 from Potters Bar to Chingford, which was a reversal since it had been lost to London Transport some years earlier. London Country put some new Olympians on the route, operated from Hatfield. They also won a route in central London with the P4 from Brixton to Lewisham which they ran with Leyland Nationals based at National Travel's Catford garage. Later that year, London Country also won tenders for the 127, 127A and 268, all former Central Area routes, the 127 being operated with a batch of nine-year-old second hand Atlanteans purchased from Southdown. Later the tender for the suburban 197/197A was won, for which London Country were able to use some of the Olympians from Godstone which were then only three years old. In the latter half of 1985, LRT also announced that many other former London Transport suburban routes would be tendered, together with a further ten central routes. In a repeat of London Transport's 1966 'Reshaping London's Buses' plan, these were to be *short, easily operated standalone routes* and would start early in 1986. By the end of 1985, LRT had put around 5% of route mileage out to tender, forecasting that within a further three years, this would rise to 25%, providing opportunities for many operators and setting in train a process which put London Buses (as London Transport's bus operation was by then known) under great pressure as they began to lose routes over which they had enjoyed a

50-year monopoly. There was generally insufficient money in a tender to finance new vehicles, so that LRT's programme created a significant increase in the second hand market. At the time though, continuing country-wide service cuts meant that redundant, relatively new second hand buses could be obtained cheaply. London Country was able to expand its fleet with numbers of these as it won various tenders, and during 1986 purchased no fewer than 62 second-hand Atlanteans with a variety of bodywork from Southdown, Strathclyde PTE, Greater Manchester and Northern General.

The August 1986 LRT scheme involving a complete revision of services around Orpington resulted in London Country losing much work. A new low-cost London Buses subsidiary, marketed as 'Roundabout', won routes which covered almost all of London Country's former routes into Orpington. There were six new routes with an R prefixed route number, operated with new Optare Pacers, replacing all of London Country's 431, 471 and 493. A red Optare Pacer in Sevenoaks Bus Station after the changes was a strange sight, although the three or four journeys into Sevenoaks from Knockholt Pound were a substantial reduction on London Country's previous timetable. Two weeks before the change, I took the opportunity to travel from Sevenoaks to Knockholt Pound and into Orpington on the 431 down the single track lane at Well Hill, returning on the 471 via Cudham. These routes were about the last of Dunton Green's rural operations, and in many ways those two journeys represented the end of an era.

After privatisation, London Country North East purchased some second hand long Leyland Nationals from Maidstone & District. A new livery was chosen and seemed less appropriate than the two tone green shown on the earlier pictures of SNB 265 and AN 113. It is at Chiltern Green working a journey on the rural 44 between Stevenage and Luton referred to earlier in the chapter. (Ian Pringle)

In August 1985, a manufacturing milestone was reached when the last Leyland Nationals were built. In 13 years, 7,800 had been produced and despite some mechanical issues, and the appalling basic standard of the early models, the National had been an undoubted success. What had been less successful though was the final total. When the factory began full production in 1972, it had the capacity to build up to 40 buses per week, or 2000 buses per year, but orders never reached even half of this capacity. British Leyland's early policy of 'one size fits all' had undoubtedly deterred some operators from purchasing the National, and even when such reliable models as the Bristol RE and Fleetline had ceased production, the National still did not find the number of orders originally hoped for. Nevertheless, they had been purchased new by every NBC operator except one (Oxford), together with many municipal and PTE fleets, and large numbers would enjoy a long service life. The National had been replaced by the Lynx which carried forward many of the National's technical innovations and included refinements from experience in service with the National. It was however to prove unsuccessful, for by the time the Lynx came into production, operators' purchasing policies had changed completely, and only 120 were sold in its first two years. The demand for new buses had reduced drastically, tendering was increasing the market in second hand buses, and there would be much uncertainty in operators' thinking for fleet replacement until the effects of de-regulation became better understood. London Country – having built up the largest fleet of Nationals anywhere – had also changed their priorities and the new Lynx was not an attractive proposition.

NBC's report for 1985 showed an increase in total passenger numbers for the first time in five years, with around 10 million more than 1984. Whilst this had produced a record turnover, actual profit was significantly down on the previous year after the costs associated with the preparation for privatisation (more than £100 million) were taken into account. In advance of deregulation on 26th October 1986 the report stated that 83% of all mileage had been registered as 'commercial' without requiring subsidy.

This picture perfectly illustrates the first generation of minibuses which soon came to be referred to as 'bread vans' and which many operators turned to as a method of reducing costs. London Country introduced them on Hemel Hempstead town services in 1986 and MBS 15 with an Iveco chassis and Carlyle 16 seat body was typical of many such minibuses across the country. In many cases their capacity proved to be inadequate, and the Hemel Hempstead network was converted to MCW Metroriders in 1987. (Capital Transport)

In the approach to deregulation, many operators began to turn to minibuses as a way of reducing costs. The minibus market had until this point been characterised almost entirely by small private hire companies and the self-drive hire market, but now minibus manufacturers saw an enormous potential among mainstream operators. The regulations had not been particularly prescriptive, but in 1986, specific provisions relating to minibuses were added to The Road Vehicle (Construction and Use) Regulations, replacing four previous sets of provisions which had applied only to private minibuses. A 'minibus' was now specifically defined as having no more than 16 seats. Standing passengers were permitted, but the numbers were limited by a maximum permissible gross vehicle weight (GVW), and on a 16 seat bus this was typically five standing.

They were particularly attractive for town service networks where frequencies could be increased by operating routes with much smaller and cheaper vehicles which could at the same time operate along narrower roads through housing estates where full sized buses could not. It was also possible to negotiate lower rates of pay for minibus drivers. By May 1986, the NBC reported that there were already 1,200 minibuses in service, and that this total would rise to about 3,000 by the year end. One of the first pioneering schemes was introduced by Devon General in the Torbay area, and many others soon followed. In Luton, United Counties replaced many of the town services with new minibus routes, and London Country introduced them at Hemel Hempstead and, after deregulation, in Guildford, Horsham and Hatfield.

The main chassis types were the Ford Transit, Leyland Sherpa and Iveco with the majority of bodywork by Dormobile or Carlyle. Many of the early versions were simply converted Ford or Iveco box vans with 12 or 16 seats, often referred to disparagingly as 'bread vans' due to their origin. The Sherpa was also available with a longer wheelbase on which Carlyle built a 20-seat body, which due to the maximum GVW could take only an additional two standing passengers giving a total capacity of 22. As the seating capacity exceeded the maximum of 16 for a 'minibus', this was a small bus and did not prove particularly attractive since the normal 16-seater could take five standing passengers without exceeding the GVW – only one fewer passenger yet still qualifying as a minibus.

It took time however for these initiatives to become successful as the capacity of the minibuses often proved inadequate and did not always encourage additional passengers. London Country's scheme at Hemel Hempstead had to be introduced in stages through a shortage of drivers, and the initial 16-seat buses proved too small in service. Although passenger numbers did increase on some new minibus networks, the vehicles themselves were far less comfortable and far more cramped than conventional buses, and operators began to look for alternatives which although smaller and cheaper than full-sized buses could give better passenger comfort.

There was also a financial consideration. A route operated by 16-seat minibuses on a frequent 7/8 minute headway gave a capacity of 128 passengers per hour, but the same route running to a 10-minute headway with 25-seat vehicles gave a capacity of 150. On a town service, whether the headway was 7, 8, or 10 minutes, made little difference to its attractiveness, but with 25-seat buses there was a reduction of 25% in the total number of buses and drivers required, which despite the higher capital cost of the larger 'small buses' was very worth while. Recognising an opportunity, MCW introduced their new 'Metrorider' 25-seat small city bus at the 1986 Motor Show. Optare, based in Leeds, had come from a rebirth of the famous Roe bodywork business, and introduced their 25-seat 'Pacer' in the same year. Both types proved very successful, and London Country replaced the original minibuses in Hemel Hempstead with MCW Metroriders in 1987.

As part of the process of splitting NBC companies into smaller units prior to de-regulation and privatisation, an order was issued on 13th February 1986 to break up London Country, following the division of several other companies which had already taken place. The splitting up of London Country into four separate companies came into operation on 7th September 1986, three weeks prior to 'Deregulation Day' on 26th September. Although the four companies were roughly equal geographically, London Country South East – which was soon renamed Kentish Bus – was the smallest in terms of its fleet size and revenue. On the actual date of the operational split, the total allocation across the four companies was 737 buses plus 215 coaches Monday to Friday, 641 plus 168 Saturday, and 193 plus 138 Sundays. This cannot accurately be compared to totals a few years earlier however since the addition of LRT contracted routes, various seasonal Green Line services and National Express coach work had greatly altered the balance of operations. If however buses allocated to routes gained under LRT tenders are discounted along with those on bus routes which had replaced sections of former Green Line routes, the numbers of buses remaining on what had been the Country Bus Network inherited from London Transport were 628 Monday to Friday, 531 Saturday and 156 Sunday. This makes an interesting comparison with the totals of January 1970 at the start of this book.

A significant measure of the endless route network changes throughout the previous fifteen years was that twelve garages put no buses at all out on Sundays on routes which could be considered as rural or even semi-rural. Hertford ran only three buses on the 310 trunk route to Enfield, Godstone three on the 411 Croydon to Reigate, and Hatfield would have had nothing on Sundays at all were it not for the LRT contract for the 298. Reigate's total Sunday run out on all bus

The cream and maroon livery introduced by Kentish Bus was not unattractive although perhaps the fleetname was a little extravagant. SNB 359 was renumbered 460, and is laying over at the terminus in Shoreham Village on the former 404 route which Kentish Bus renumbered 24. By the time this picture was taken, the Shoreham service had been reduced to a mere three or four journeys a day. (Ian Pringle)

The Iveco Talbot minibuses which Kentish Bus introduced after deregulation provided a hard, cramped and uncomfortable ride. Fortunately they proved to be short lived. On 22nd August 1990, 883 is in Sevenoaks bus station waiting to depart on one of the three remaining journeys to Shoreham Village. (Author)

On the Surrey/Kent border, subsidy reductions for the 464 meant that by 1984, only three journeys remained between Oxted and Chart plus a fourth on Thursday morning on the 465 'village bus' which ran down to Crockham Hill In 1985, to improve the service to Chart, a few journeys on the 410 were diverted between Limpsfield and Westerham, and in August 1987, AN 189 comes up from Kent Hatch towards Chart on a 410 to Reigate. Until 1976, this road had seen an hourly service on the 464/465 to Westerham or Edenbridge. (Author)

routes was down to just seven, while Dorking's was just the single bus for the 417 'Ramblers Bus' which ran only for the summer period and finished the week after the formal split into the four companies.

Following the split, Kentish Bus soon revised its network, renumbering routes and abandoning the traditional 400 series London Transport numbers. In May 1987, the Green Line link from Tunbridge Wells to London begun by Autocar in June 1930 was finally severed, being replaced with a bus route numbered 22 from Tunbridge Wells to Bromley. Passenger loadings on Sundays were so poor that Kentish Bus could not run the route commercially on that day, so registered it only on weekdays. Kent County Council therefore had to subsidise the Sunday service and put it out to tender, operation being won by Maidstone Corporation (or Boro'line as it was by then known). This illustrated the anomalies which deregulation would throw up since this involved Maidstone running dead mileage to take up service, but presumably still cheaper than Kentish Bus even though Dunton Green garage was on the line of the route. Kentish Bus also introduced minibuses in the form of six-wheel Iveco Talbots branded as 'Kentish Hopper' with angular bodies, and a level of passenger comfort which was just as awful as the original Leyland Nationals. The leg room was so limited that an average person could not sit properly in the seats, and the ride quality was hard and bouncy. They proved to be short-lived. Prior to deregulation, Swanley garage had been closed in January 1986, but re-opened six months later as an outstation to Dartford when the LRT contract to run the 51 route was won. When the contract for the route came up for renewal however, Kentish Bus was unsuccessful and Swanley closed again in August 1989.

In the period running up to deregulation, operators had to decide which routes (or parts of routes or individual journeys) they were prepared to register commercially, the remainder being left to local authorities to tender as they saw fit. So great were the numbers of tenders that, in a repeat of the problems of the early days of subsidy applications, local authorities had insufficient time and resources

The introduction of the 379 in May 1975 resurrected a service through Bramfield and Datchworth four years after the 329 had been withdrawn. Despite many routes lost by London Country at deregulation, the 379 was retained, and on Friday 24th April 1987, SNB 265 comes down the lane through the woods from Bulls Green towards Bramfield on the 1.10pm from Stevenage. The bus has been repainted into the North East livery adopted after London Country was split and a year later the Company would be the last of all the former NBC subsidiaries to be sold. (Author)

to conclude them all before deregulation, or to give operators sufficient notice to organise resources. This made it difficult for operators to plan numbers of vehicles and drivers to run any new contracts. Such a situation arose when London Country did not register the 708 Green Line route beyond Hemel Hempstead, leaving the section on to Aylesbury potentially withdrawn. The tender process led to a delay in introducing a replacement service, which was won by Marshall's coaches of Leighton Buzzard and had the effect of cutting the previous service into two sections.

London Country experienced many changes in the period approaching deregulation. In January 1985, well before deregulation, Hertfordshire's need to reduce subsidies had already resulted in the 317 being transferred to B&B Coaches, who ran another route between Hemel Hempstead and Berkhamsted. After Tring garage had shut, the remote operation of the 387 Tring to Aldbury route had become increasingly expensive for London Country, so at the same time it went to Red Rover who were able to run it at much less cost. In a similar transfer, the 392 and 393 (Welwyn Garden City – Hertford – Harlow) went to Golden Boy Coaches in August 1985. London Country also wanted to withdraw the 501 to Ongar at the same time, so Golden Boy agreed to extend part of the 392/393 from Harlow to Epping and Ongar.

Deregulation itself brought about many further changes in Hertfordshire. London Country registered only five peak journeys on the 341 between Hertford and Hatfield, the hourly service during the day being won by Eastern National who had to run buses remotely from their nearest depot at Bishop's Stortford. They had wanted to run over London Country's 350/351 from Bishops Stortford to Hertford which would have substantially reduced the costs of positioning buses for the 341, but this was won in a separate tender by Reg's Coaches who had also won the works journeys on the 315 to Kimpton. Reg's also won part of the 390 between Stevenage and Hertford after London Country registered only a handful of commercial journeys. United Counties won some works journeys on the 303C from Stevenage factory area to Hitchin, and took back the 314 from Hitchin to Welwyn Garden City. London Country did not register the Stevenage to Letchworth route, but still won the tender for this, setting up a new route numbered 323. In a reversal however, it did win the tenders for some minor rural routes east of Harlow which Eastern National had run since the 1930s but did not register. One of these ironically saw London Country serve the hamlet of Toothill again which it had abandoned some 16 years earlier, albeit only two days a week. The Friday journey on the 386 from Hertford to Stevenage went to Smiths who started the journey from Cottered, but extended it back to Buntingford when Cottered village shop closed in July 1987. Some of the 352 journeys out to the village of Bucks Hill were won by an independent, but they failed after a year, London Country winning them in the re-tender.

A more positive aspect of the deregulated competitive market was illustrated In Welwyn Garden City and Hatfield. London Country had not registered their former 'G' town services commercially and they had been taken over by Sampson Coaches in a tender. In August 1987 a new company called 'Welwyn Hatfield Line' was set up by some former London Country drivers, who purchased 11 new Optare Pacers and set up a brand new network in direct competition to Sampson. Their new buses and generally attractive fares were sufficient to make the new venture a success to the extent that Sampson withdrew from the two towns in the face of Welwyn Hatfield Line's competition.

London Country was more fortunate in west Hertfordshire, where they won the tenders for almost all of the services they had not registered, in particular around Watford and Hemel Hempstead. They also won the tender for the United Counties route from Hemel Hempstead to Dunstable which had replaced their own 337 in 1972 after they had withdrawn in the face of a lack of subsidy from Bedfordshire. In Buckinghamshire however, London Country were unable to register the majority of the rural routes around Chesham and Amersham, and the routes to St Leonards, Buckland Common and Tring were won by Red Rover who purchased some new Optare Pacers to run them.

At first, London Country North West made no change to the livery other than to remove the NBC double arrow and add 'North West' in smaller letters under the fleetname. AN 65 still carries the 'Watford Wide' branding as it stops at Watford Junction on a 321 to Maple Cross. (Ian Pringle)

London Country North West later applied this livery, and LR 73 makes an interesting comparison to AN 65 on the previous page. It has stopped in the same place working a 321 to Luton. The running number is slotted in behind the front windscreen next to a board with the North West fleetname. (Ian Pringle)

One change which certainly disadvantaged the travelling public occurred in the Slough town service network. While London Country registered the routes commercially, on Sundays they registered only half of the previous timetables. Bucks County Council were not prepared to subsidise the unregistered half, and since other operators would not have wished to run in direct competition with London Country – in a classic example of unintended consequences – the Sunday timetables were effectively halved.

Following deregulation, Surrey looked again at the area to the west of Kingston, and in early 1987 put most routes out to tender, proposing revisions which would cause great conflict. London Buses proposed setting up a complete new low-cost subsidiary to compete for the routes, to be called 'Kingston Buses'. Norbiton garage would be closed, all its staff being given redundancy notices, and told that they could apply to join Kingston Buses on new contracts at lower rates of pay. The Unions took London Buses to court but lost, and many disillusioned staff simply left. To minimise costs, Kingston Buses needed second hand buses but insufficient re-certified DMSs were available in time, and the new network suffered significant problems, illustrating in the process some of the negative

For a short period, Surrey County Council supported a limited Sunday service on the Dorking to Guildford route. Surrey's policy was to number their subsidised routes in the 500 series, so the former 425 route number was the basis for the 525. London Country South West converted AN 125 to open top, and repainted it into this attractive green and yellow livery for use on the route on fine summer Sundays, and is laying over at Dorking station waiting to work to Guildford on just such a day. (Ian Pringle)

aspects of tendering and deregulation. London Country South West however won more work by taking over the 131 (Wimbledon – Hampton Court – Walton) using second hand Atlanteans purchased from Greater Manchester which they operated from Addlestone and Leatherhead.

Deregulation also led to some direct competition just as the legislation envisaged. In February 1987, C&S Coaches started a route from Harefield to Uxbridge in competition with the long standing 347, and Eastern National registered a service between Bishop's Stortford and Epping to compete with London Country. London Buses started a route between Enfield and Hertford, which they numbered 310A in direct competition with the existing 310. London Country North East soon countered by registering a second route numbered 510 with buses timed to run just six minutes ahead of the London Buses route. These were examples of hundreds of similar competitive services registered all over the country as operators hoped to take advantage of profitable routes. All too often however, the result was an over-provision which meant that nobody made any real profit and large numbers of the new competitive services did not last long, adding to public inconvenience and uncertainty. There were some less savoury incidents of large operators introducing routes in direct competition with an existing operator, running just in front of the existing timetable, often with greatly reduced or even free fares. Some of these were undoubtedly of questionable legality and were deliberately intended to drive away the original operator, but proved to be isolated abuses of the new legislation.

In the first year or two after deregulation, the changes in routes, timetables, and operators across what had been the 'Country Bus Area' would fill a book on their own. The changes illustrated just how much bus operation was affected by the new regime and the great uncertainty which would continue for a few years until more settled networks were established. During 1987, the four separated London Country companies were prepared for sale, and on 5th January 1988 London Country North West was the first to be sold off and privatised. The remaining three followed quickly with London Country North East being the last

on 22nd April 1988, and in fact the last of all the former NBC subsidiaries to be sold. In some instances, NBC had to be prepared to consider 'negative bids' – i.e. to pay someone to take over a company. With little or no property (NBC had transferred ownership of most of the offices and garages to a separate property company), many of the actual bus operating businesses had no tangible assets. They could be profitable only with continuing subsidy in a market where the continuation of any company's route network was not a certainty, since it might gain or lose work frequently in tendering, and any profitable commercial routes might be subject to competition from another operator at any time. London Country North West fell into this 'negative bid' category, but in the final analysis privatisation was successfully completed.

Newly won tenders rarely included enough return to purchase new buses, and a thriving market in second hand double deckers soon developed. London Country purchased several Atlanteans from Greater Manchester PTE and made good use of their destination displays which had been unique to the old Manchester Corporation fleet and carried on into later designs. On 3rd June 1989 – the day of my last ever Green Rover – AN 365 picks up in Redhill Bus Station. (Author)

After Privatisation and the split of London Country, Green Line services continued to be operated by the four separate companies. The remaining routes in Surrey were heavily subsidised by Surrey County Council, and in June 1991, four years after London Country South East came into being, Surrey discontinued their support leading to the withdrawal of the 714 and 715. On the 714, the Dorking to Horsham section was replaced by an hourly bus route numbered 93 and the section from Kingston to Dorking by extending London Buses 265 route from Chessington. On 28th June 1991, the last day of operation, TP 17 comes through Mickleham Village from Burford Bridge at Boxhill on the 9.00am 714 from Horsham. The hourly headway between Dorking and Leatherhead on the 714 was all that remained of a service which once consisted of four Green Line coaches an hour all day seven days a week plus two or three 470s every hour. Added to this were many weekend Green Line duplicates and a 20 or 30 minute Summer Sunday headway on central route 93 until 1960. Boxhill had been one of the main attractions in the Country Bus area and this picture, representing the last day of a once busy route, is a fitting end to this book. (Author)

In the next few years, operators everywhere would survive or fail on their ability to keep costs to a minimum and constantly review each route to ensure it remained worth while. Those management teams who could achieve this often sold on their companies at some profit, while large groups such as Stagecoach, Arriva, First and Go-Ahead would gradually acquire companies to form large and successful operations with economies of scale and the sort of low-cost base and flexible, imaginative management of which London Transport was never capable.

As discussed at the beginning of this book, London Transport's management with its inflexibility and inadequate response to changing social and economic times had undoubtedly made a bad situation worse, particularly during the 1960s. But London Transport was by no means an exception. The whole industry, the large majority of which was also wholly or partly State or Local Authority owned, was equally slow to react and change operating practices which were too often – like the railways – based on over-manning and outdated and inflexible working arrangements. The cumbersome and over-bureaucratic licensing system and Traffic Courts were also factors in preventing rapid changes to routes and time-tables, and the Trade Unions through their implacable resistance to change had also been a further significant factor in the financial decline of the bus industry. Richard Beeching is often remembered as someone who did irreparable damage to the railway network, but by the 1960s more than 90% of British Railways' fare revenue came from less than 10% of train miles run, and not a single branch line station took enough in fares even to pay the wages of the station staff, never mind a contribution to rolling stock, tracks and signalling. Even the Labour Government of the time recognised that the huge losses were unsustainable, and Beeching

chose the only commercial option open to him at the time, stripping away old working practices and overmanning, and closing loss-making routes en-masse. It would be interesting to speculate what might have happened if a similar appointment had been made in the 1960s to 'head up' Britain's bus companies. Perhaps deregulation, competition and privatisation might have come 20 years earlier than it did – we shall never know!

The four former London Country companies would go through many further changes both in routes and ownership. Cost reductions and the harsher commercial climate of competition led to the closure of garages at St Albans, Amersham and Hertford in 1989, Chelsham, Godstone, and Dorking in 1990, and Stevenage in 1991. Twenty years earlier when London Country had taken over, the notion of closing any of these would have seemed impossible. Later on even 'Headquarters' at Reigate was closed as fleets became smaller and were dispersed to 'low cost' operating bases, often no more than open parking yards with a 'Portakabin' for an office and staff rest room. Routine maintenance could be sub-contracted to local companies at much less cost than maintaining the overhead of a garage and all its staff.

In June 1989, I went on what would be my last 'Green Rover' from Godstone through Reigate, Dorking and Guildford, via Ewhurst to Cranleigh on down to Horsham and back via Crawley and East Grinstead. The day was spent mostly on Leyland Nationals and Atlanteans with an Olympian from Reigate to Dorking and an Iveco minibus from Dorking to Guildford. The day had been quite difficult to plan, given the lower frequency of the timetables, but it covered many of the routes I had travelled so many times on RTs, RFs and GSs. It had been 27 years since my first London Transport 'Green Rover' and during that time I had travelled over every single deck route – in some cases many times – together with most of the main trunk routes, and even some of the town services. Even in 1962 when my travels had begun, the old Country Bus area was still buoyant, loadings were high, and the network was run by people who had some pride in what they did. Not long before the Green Line network was rescued from complete failure in 1977, I had travelled on a 727 from Kingston to St Albans on a scruffy Leyland National driven by a man with tattooed arms wearing trainers, jeans and a short sleeved T shirt with a football club logo. He clearly had no interest whatsoever in his job or his passengers, and both he and the bus demonstrated just how far London Transport's once high standards had fallen. That London Country eventually restored much of the damage was to their great credit, but in the end commercial reality and social change led to the inevitable break up and the end of bus services as they had existed for more than half a century.

In the case of London Transport's old Country Bus area, the buses would become 'Green No More'. As I wrote in my introduction, I am just glad that I was able to travel round the 'Country Area' when I did!

BIBLIOGRAPHY

Information about the history of London Transport's Country Buses and London Country Bus Services can be found in a number of books, magazines and publications. In addition to my own recollections and records, I have used many sources for this book in my attempt to write the story of how the Country Area declined to the point of virtual bankruptcy, to eventually be resurrected by London Country and changed forever.

The following sources have all provided information.

- Buses Illustrated and Buses magazines from the late 1950s onwards. Many articles, too many to list, which have provided information.
- The Transport Act 1980 – HMSO 1980
- Fleet History LT12 (single deck vehicles) – The PSV Circle 1995
- Several LOTS Publications including :-

    SUP 19   RT Demise by Les Stitson

    SUP 9   London Country Allocations 1st January 1970

    TEX 3   London Country Allocations 1971, 1972, 1973

    SUP   London Country Allocations & Route Workings 1974-85

    The London Bus Review 1978, 1980, 1981, and 1982
- London Country Bus Services – various traffic circulars 1970-1972
- Reshaping London's Bus Services – London Transport 1966
- London Country – edited by David Stewart, Capital Transport 1984
- London Country in the 1970s – Steve Fennell, Ian Allan Publishing 2003
- RT – Ken Blacker, Capital Transport 1980
- RF – Ken Glazier, Capital Transport 1991
- London Country – John Glover, Ian Allan 2006
- Routemaster Vol 2 1970-1989 – Ken Blacker, Capital Transport 1992
- The British Bus Story 1970s – The Proof of the Pudding. Alan Townsin, Transport Publishing 1987
- London Transport Garages – Ken Glazier, Capital Transport 2006
- ECW 1965-1987. Maurice Doggett and Alan Townsin. Venture 1994
- RT Family Garage Allocations volume 2 – Stuart Robbs Publishing 2002
- Tillingbourne – George Burnett & Laurie James, Middleton Press 1990
- London Transport Connections 1945-1985 – Philip Wallis, Capital Transport 2003
- Green Line 1930-1980 – D.W.K. Jones & B.J.Davis, London Country Bus Services 1980
- Single Deck Garage Allocations RF; MB; SM. Stewart Robbs 2016